Synthesizing
Family,
Career,
AND
Culture

A Model
for
Counseling
in the
Twenty-First Century

Edited by

Kathy M. Evans
Joseph C. Rotter
Joshua M. Gold

5999 Stevenson Avenue
Alexandria, VA 22304
www.counseling.org

Synthesizing
Family,
Career,
AND
Culture

∽

A Model for Counseling in the Twenty-First Century

10   9   8   7   6   5   4   3   2   1

American Counseling Association
5999 Stevenson Avenue
Alexandria, VA 22304
www.counseling.org

Director of Publications • Carolyn C. Baker

Production Manager • Bonny Gaston

Copy Editor • Elaine Dunn

Cover Design • Jennifer Arbaiza

Library of Congress Cataloging-in-Publication Data

Synthesizing family, career, and culture : a model for counseling in the twenty-first century / edited by Kathy M. Evans, Joseph C. Rotter, Joshua M. Gold.
    p. cm.
Includes bibliographical references and index.
    ISBN 1-55620-193-1 (alk. paper)
    1. Family counseling.   2. Cross-cultural counseling.   3. Vocational guidance.   I. Title: Family, career, and culture.   II. Evans, Kathy M.
III. Rotter, Joseph C.   VI. Gold, Joshua M. (Joshua Mark).
    HV697 .S96 2002
    362.82′86—dc21   2002020512

❧ Table of Contents ❧

❧ Part I ❧

Philosophical Rationale

❧ Part II ❧

Theoretical Perspectives

❧ Part III ❧

Treatment Strategies

❧ Part IV ❦
New Directions

ᴖ Preface ᴓ

Career and work constitute a major portion of most people's lives, families have an impact on people's careers, and their culture determines a great deal about how they approach family and work. Until now, the family counseling literature has given little attention to work, the career literature has given little attention to families, and the multicultural literature has given only glancing reference to either family or career issues. It is our hope that *Synthesizing Family, Career, and Culture* will help counselors integrate these three areas that are so segmented in the profession.

We believe that this book will be particularly helpful to graduate students in helping professions, faculty of those programs, and professionals who are currently delivering counseling services. In over 300 counseling programs, students receive instruction in career counseling, multicultural counseling, and family counseling in separate courses, and they are responsible for integrating these three areas of study. This book assists students in this endeavor and helps faculty in the Council for Accreditation of Counseling and Related Education Programs (CACREP) and those seeking to become CACREP accredited meet the standard that specifies not only that students understand the interrelationships among and between work, family, and other life roles but also that they understand the influence of diversity and gender on career development. Moreover, this book presents a rationale for approaching career, multicultural, and family orientations that transcends theoretical approaches by offering examples of application. Professionals in the helping fields, therefore, would find the book attractive for meeting the needs of their clients, continuing education, and in-service training.

We combine theory and practice in this text because we believe it is the best way to present a process model such as ours. Part I: Philosophical Rationale is designed to give the reader some background on how the out-of-the-box model came about. In chapter 1, Rotter and Evans explore the rationale for combining the concepts of family, career, and multicultural counseling and set the stage for the remaining chapters of the book.

In Part II: Theoretical Perspectives, we examine theoretical perspectives and their influences on the new model. First, chapter 2 presents our model for counseling in the 21st century. We have named it the *out-of-the-box model* because we are encouraging counselors to reach out beyond their stated specializations and to develop fluency in family, culture, and career counseling. Next, in chapter 3, Murray et al. review the popular theories of career and family counseling and critique them regarding their inclusion of all three perspectives: family, culture, and career. This chapter also emphasizes the importance of career assessment in theory development and practice.

Part III: Treatment Strategies focuses on practical applications. We devised three case studies of fictionalized clients who were based on real clients we have seen. In chapter 4, Ochs and Evans approach the first case study and apply the model to counseling an individual. In their approach, they show how to equally apply a career and a family counseling theory to work within the out-of-the-box model. Snow and Carlson apply the model to the second case study in chapter 5. They not only illustrate how the model can be used by counselors to guide their thinking about how to approach client problems but also show how Adlerian theory can be adapted to it. In chapter 6, Foster, Eriksen, and McAuliffe incorporate a feminist perspective into the out-of-the-box framework. They address numerous internal and external influences associated with gender bias and sex role socialization, including gender oppression, heterosexual presumption, racism, and sex role stereotyping.

Finally, Part IV: New Directions is devoted to the directions we need to take as a profession. In chapter 7, Hawley, Goodman, and Shaieb address the research that exists and that is still needed to inform our practice of family, career, and multicultural counseling. In chapter 8, Jencius reviews ethical guidelines and standards of practice and training to discover the converging themes and the adaptations needed for counselors and counselors-in-training to embrace the model.

It is our hope that after reading this work, you will agree that we can no longer consider the individual as an island but must consider the contributions of his or her unique cultural and familial contexts in his or her lifestyle development. Rather than continue to ignore the interconnections of culture, family, and career, all are recognized as directing the individual in unique ways. This book, of course, is not the penultimate statement regarding this topic. Because of the limits of space, we have only scratched the surface. We leave the reader to explore further the implications. The dawning of the 21st century is an excellent time to initiate a new approach to counseling that better meets the needs and demands of an ever-changing society.

❦ Acknowledgments ❧

We would like to thank Gretchen Morris for her assistance in gathering information, organizing our work, and spending countless hours in the library and searching databases. We are also indebted to Becky Wilson for her excellent work in creating the graphics for our out-of-the-box model. Finally, we are very grateful to Carolyn Baker for her helpful feedback as well as her support and encouragement during the process of completing this project.

৯ About the Editors ৩

Kathy M. Evans, PhD, is an associate professor in the Department of Educational Psychology at the University of South Carolina. She received her PhD from the Pennsylvania State University and is a National Certified Counselor. Dr. Evans has over 25 publications and has presented at over 50 national, regional, and local professional conferences. Her research, publications, and teaching focus on multicultural, career, and women's issues in training counselors.

Joseph C. Rotter, EdD, is a professor in the Department of Educational Psychology at the University of South Carolina. He is a National Certified Counselor, Licensed Professional Counselor Supervisor, and Licensed Counseling Psychologist. He has served a 3-year term as editor of the *Elementary School Guidance and Counseling* journal and currently serves as associate editor of *The Family Journal*. Dr. Rotter is also co-author of five books and many articles in professional journals. He is past president of the Association for Counselor Education and Supervision.

Joshua M. Gold, PhD, NCC, is an associate professor of Counselor Education at the University of South Carolina. He is a clinical member and approved supervisor of the American Association of Marriage and Family Therapy. His emphasis in teaching and research is in the area of family counseling and the integration between family counseling and other counseling specializations.

❧ About the Contributors ❧

Kimberly Boudrot, EdS, is currently a doctoral student in Counselor Education completing her studies at the University of South Carolina and is an elementary school counselor.

Jon Carlson, PsyD, EdD, ABPP, is a professor of Psychology and Counseling at Governors State University and psychologist at the Lake Geneva (Wisconsin) Wellness Clinic. He has authored 25 books, over 100 articles, and developed over 100 professional video programs. He has been president of the International Association of Marriage and Family Counselors and serves as editor of *The Family Journal*.

Karen Eriksen, PhD, teaches at Radford University, graduated from George Mason University, and serves in leadership in a number of state and national professional associations. Her research focuses on counselor competency and adult development. She has published three books on counselor education.

Victoria Foster, EdD, is an associate professor in Counselor Education and the director of the New Horizons Family Counseling Center at the College of William and Mary.

Jane Goodman, PhD, is an associate professor of Counseling at Oakland University. She is the 2001–2002 president of the American Counseling Association and a past president of the Michigan Counseling Association and the National Career Development Association. She is author of many articles and book chapters, primarily in the area of career development of adults.

Lisa D. Hawley, PhD, is an assistant professor of Counseling at Oakland University. Her areas of research include issues related to culture, group work, and supervision. She is currently affiliated with the American Counseling Association and Michigan Counseling Association.

Marty Jencius earned his PhD in Counselor Education from the University of South Carolina and is an assistant professor at Kent State

University. He is founder of CESNET-L, a listserv for counselor educators and cofounding editor of *The Journal of Technology in Counseling*. His interests include the use of technology in counseling and instructional methods in multicultural counseling.

Garrett McAuliffe, PhD, is a faculty member in the Counseling Program at Old Dominion University. He has been a practicing licensed counselor specializing in career issues. His doctoral work in career development won the national award for outstanding dissertation.

Patricia Murray, MA, LPC, NCC, is a doctoral student completing her studies in Counselor Education at the University of South Carolina. Additionally, she is employed as a college counselor at Gardner-Webb University. Her research interests are in creative techniques in counseling, supervision, and working with student athletes.

Nancy Ochs received her EdD from the College of William and Mary. She has worked in public mental health clinics as a child and family therapist and is currently a member of ReSource Therapy Associates, a private mental health practice and wellness center in Reston, Virginia. Nancy combines interests in multicultural issues, White racial issues, developing therapeutic games for children, brief therapy, and eye-movement desensitization response applications.

Erika Reents, MA, is a doctoral student completing her studies in Counselor Education at the University of South Carolina. She is an elementary school counselor and has been for 8 years. She also works at Clemson Community Clinic in Clemson, South Carolina. Her research interests involve issues for working with children and supervision of counselors.

Tamara Roberts, MA, is currently a doctoral student in Counselor Education completing her studies at the University of South Carolina and is on the administrative staff of South Carolina State University.

Mary Shaieb, MA, LPC, is a doctoral student completing her studies in Counseling at Oakland University. Mary has a strong research, clinical, and teaching background in the area of career and transition. She is also involved in the Adult Career Counseling Center and various other local agencies.

Kim Snow, MA, LCPC, is an adjunct professor of Counseling at Governors State University and a counselor at Oak Lawn Family Services Agency in Illinois. In addition to working with Dr. Carlson on various video projects and articles, she enjoys spending time with her six children and her husband, Cy.

Laurie Williamson, EdD, LPC, ACS, is an assistant professor in the Department of Human Development and Psychological Counseling at Appalachia State University.

Part I

ᛋ

Philosophical
Rationale

❧ Chapter 1 ❧

The Influence of Family, Career, and Culture on Individuals

Joseph C. Rotter and Kathy M. Evans

James and Tamisha Simmons, an African American couple, have lived in a small rural town of 1,200 people all their lives. Until recently, they both worked in the community. However, the textile plant, which employed many townspeople, closed, forcing many adults to seek employment at a resort island some 1½ hours away. James and Tamisha have two young children ages 4 and 7. Fortunately, since very few young people leave the community, there is a sense of family where pooling of resources and a strong support system are in place. Tamisha's grandmother cares for the children before and after school since Tamisha and her husband work on the island until 5:00 p.m. 6 days a week. Given the distance to work, both James and Tamisha must leave the house by 6:00 a.m. to catch the bus to the island and they don't return home until 7:30 in the evening. And, depending on traffic and weather, it can be at times much later in the evening. Tamisha and James are working as housekeeper and grounds maintenance respectively at one of the island hotels. Needless to say, their combined income is barely over the poverty level. They want the best for their children but are concerned that the children may fall into the same trap as they if they do not leave the community. This is a dilemma for James and Tamisha, because family is important and they fear that if they or the children should leave town, they may never return.

The ever-changing family structure and the changing work roles of the client population in the United States are reasons enough for changing the approach to counseling to a more multifaceted and inclusive one that involves culture, family, and career. Some would argue that career implies culture and family, and this very well might be so. However, in practice, given the specialty nature of counseling, we as

3

counselors tend to compartmentalize family, career, and culture as if they were separate entities. This chapter introduces the concept of synthesizing the roles of career, family, and culture in the process of career choice. The scenario cited above is but one of an unlimited number of family, career, and cultural combinations. As we develop the model presented in this book, you will be exposed to other familial examples, although these examples by no means cover the gambit of family configurations and related issues. It is hoped that you will be able to extrapolate from these examples and the presented model a frame of reference for your own practice.

❧ Historical Perspective ❧

The notion that families influence career choice is not a new concept. From the beginning of time, children have entered the family business. There have been generations of business owners, farmers, doctors, nurses, teachers, and lawyers. Hotchkiss and Borow (1990) pointed out that the sociological effect of career status is passed from generation to generation and is reinforced by the child's contact with significant other adults in the same social stratum. In fact, family dynamics and career decision making have been found to be related (Kinnier, Brigman, & Noble, 1990). According to Rockwell (1987), individuals make career decisions with the expectation of receiving the approval of significant others (e.g., family members). Gottfredson (1981) theorized that family-determined socially acceptable career choices are among the last factors to be compromised when an individual makes career decisions. Further evidence of support for the inclusion of family in counseling is that systems theories have been generally accepted in counseling and psychology as a means to understand the individual in the context of his or her social environment. Interestingly, there is little literature that addresses the phenomenon of family influence on career choice and career decision making. A leading text in multicultural family counseling by McGoldrick, Giordano, and Pearce (1996) includes only the briefest mention of career issues for a few ethnic groups. Although many career counseling texts make minor mention of family, much of career counseling has an individual focus. Usually the career counselor helps the client explore his or her interests, abilities, values, and needs with family issues as a lesser concern. This focus is problematic for many ethnic groups and is particularly so for ethnic minority groups, for whom the rule, rather than the exception, is that group needs outweigh individual interests, wants, or needs.

Multicultural family counseling requires a redefinition of the word *family*. For many ethnic populations in the United States, a family is more than a father, mother, and their children. It often includes extended family (grandparents, aunts, uncles, and cousins), close family friends in the community, and ancestors and all their descendants (Lee, 1999; McGoldrick et al., 1996). With respect to ethnic minority clients, Paniagua (1996) recommended that rather than provide a definition of family, it is better for family therapists to let their clients define the significant people in their lives whom they consider family members.

Rowland (1991) argued that the typical family life cycle has been disrupted by social changes including, but not limited to, single-parent families, dual-career/earner families, blended families, and extended families. The family life cycle illustrated by Carter and McGoldrick (1988) can provide the family therapist with points of entry where career issues may become significant. For example, as young couples begin to establish a life together, they may also be launching careers that demand a considerable amount of their time and can contribute to the stress manifested during the time they are together. When children enter the scene, often the career of one of the adults is curtailed, thus creating the potential for further stress. As the temporarily at-home parent returns to the work world or continues his or her education, new stresses are encountered. Issues of separation, realignment of family roles, misunderstandings regarding changes in emphasis from home to work for the parent returning to work, insecurities related to the changing roles, particularly reentry into the job market or return to school, can create stress within the family. In midlife, adults retiring from the workforce may be struggling with adjustments to a new lifestyle. And the cycle continues. Launching one's own children into the work world can be traumatic for families who are dealing with separation and security issues. Referencing the example at the beginning of this chapter, adding culture to this mix only compounds the cycle. For example, not all families follow this "cookie-cutter" life-cycle formula. Today many women return to work without extensive absence after delivering a child. In other cases, the father becomes the stay-at-home parent. Many families have just one parent. And in other families, it is important for the children to find work while in school to help support the family.

Regardless of the family configuration or cultural influences on family life, issues regarding work and career enter into the picture at some point. It is important for the therapist to be sensitive to these cultural differences and acknowledge the influences that they have on one's career development. Cultural sensitivity is the basis for multicultural career counseling, which involves the application of multicultural principles to the practice of career counseling.

Although career is defined as the dependent variable in the mix in the model described in chapter 2, multicultural competence is the backdrop for family career counseling. In fact, most of the strategies recommended in book chapters and journal articles reflect the multicultural competencies published by the Association for Multicultural Counseling and Development (Arredondo et al., 1996). The competencies are divided into three areas of counselor sensitivity: (a) counselor awareness of his or her own cultural values and biases, (b) counselor knowledge of the client's worldview, and (c) culturally appropriate intervention strategies. The competencies are operationally defined in the document and are intended to help counselors best serve their clients, whatever the client's cultural background or presenting problem.

An integrated theoretical approach to career counseling that involves notions of not only decision making but also development and self-concept would increase understanding and facilitate the use of the multicultural competencies with ethnically diverse populations. For example, Gottfredson's (1981) theory of circumscription could enhance understanding of the limited career choices of some ethnic minority group members; Super's (1985) theory explains other choices for ethnic minority group members by showing that societal influences may hinder the development of one's self-concept through the work one chooses; and Krumboltz's (1994) social learning theory of career development, in which individuals benefit from vicarious learning and learn from the environment, would all be useful in counseling families about careers. Family systems theories are also amenable to the application of career counseling from a multicultural perspective. Herr and Cramer (1996) stated:

> Whether from a contextual, sociological, or a situational perspective, the family is a facilitator of experiences that expand or limit family members' knowledge of occupations, a reinforcement system of contingencies and expectations that subtly or directly shape work behavior, and a purveyor of socioeconomic status. The home is itself a workplace and a center in which social and occupational roles are modeled either by the members of the nuclear family or the network of friends and acquaintances with which this unit interacts. (p. 206)

Herring (1998) devoted a chapter in his book, *Career Counseling in Schools: Multicultural and Developmental Perspectives*, to family influences on career development. He outlined important background information about ethnic minority families for career counselors, including socioeconomic status, poverty, parental education, parental occupations, language barriers, intergenerational conflicts, and grandparents performing as parents. In addition to the factors listed by Herring, job discrimination, cultural child-rearing practices, and cultural career expectations related to gender and age are also important. Although no complete book addresses this issue, there are several recent book chapters devoted to multicultural family career counseling, family and career counseling, or multicultural career counseling (Herring, 1998; Lee, 1999; Patton & McMahon, 1999; Peterson & Gonzalez, 2000; Sharf, 1997; Zunker, 1998).

℘ Issues Specific to Multicultural Families and Career Development ❦

Outlined below are some of the issues that counselors encounter most often when working with ethnic minority group families. Our definition of a multicultural family includes those that are ethnic minority group members, families that are racially blended through adoption, and families that are bicultural or bicultural through intermarriage. Not all families have all of these problems. There may be some families that have none of these problems, but the issues are important enough that the discussion of multicultural family career counseling would be incomplete without addressing them.

Socioeconomic Status

Herr and Cramer (1996) stated that social class is more of an influence on career development than race and ethnicity and, in fact, accounts for most of the differences between groups. Children, regardless of race, who grow up with a higher socioeconomic status have higher educational achievement and get better jobs (Friesen, 1986). Families with a higher socioeconomic status are more likely to have the resources needed to provide the education necessary for high-status occupations. Poverty is an overwhelming issue for ethnic minority groups because they are overrepresented among the poor. Families living in poverty experience a number of career-related problems, most of which are the result of limited or low levels of education. Unemployment, underemployment, and employment in insecure, low-level jobs with few, if any, benefits are often the reality for most individuals living in poverty. Consequently, they develop negative feelings about the world of work such as a lack of hope, belief in the future, and self-confidence. Children sensitive to their parents' feelings and beliefs go on to internalize these attitudes as well. Weinger (1998) found that poor children believe that they are treated unfairly by society, that opportunities are designed for the nonpoor, that they may not achieve even their scaled-down career choices, and that they will not have the skills and know-how that middle-class and upper-class children have.

Language Barriers

Even families who may not be impoverished can experience language-related barriers. Immigrants and U.S. citizens who do not speak standard

English may have difficulties with work as the inability to speak fluent standard English results in many occupational opportunities being closed to them. However, once an individual becomes bilingual, she or he will find that the ability to speak more than one language is a huge asset in the work world.

Generational Conflicts

Generational conflicts are most evident in families who have immigrated with their young children or whose children have been born in the United States. In some of these families, the culture in the home is more likely to resemble the family's country of origin than the culture in the United States, and the difference between the two cultures presents problems. Herring (1998) stated that the essential problem is the ongoing acculturation process or the rejection of parental career aspirations for their children (p. 210). The children easily take on the values and attitudes of the dominant culture while the parents may resist such acculturation (Rotter & Hawley, 1998). The resulting conflicts can seriously affect family functioning as well as the career development of the child.

Other generational issues include grandparents who act in place of parents who are unable to raise their children themselves. Because there is such a large gap in the experiences of these two generations, grandparents may offer career advice that may be outdated and possibly hinder the child's career development.

Discrimination

Racial discrimination is most likely the second most devastating factor influencing the career development of ethnic minority groups after poverty. Discrimination has affected career aspirations and choice, career advancement, and career satisfaction. It is evidenced by the fact that racial and ethnic minority group members hold only 10% of the managerial and 13% of the professional positions in the United States even though they make up more than 30% of the population (Gysbers, Heppner, & Johnston, 1998, p. 35). How a person perceives the possibility of employment discrimination affects his or her attitudes, values, and behavior toward work (Herr & Cramer, 1996). Needless to say, adults and children alike need to learn coping behaviors when it comes to living in a society that discriminates against them. Most families are equipped to work with their children on this issue but some are not.

❧ Issues for European American Families ❧

European Americans (Whites) make up the largest cultural group in the United States. However, when culture is addressed, we focus on ethnic minorities and often leave out a discussion of White Americans. In fact, multicultural trainers report that Whites themselves often state that they do not have a culture. McGoldrick and Giordano (1996) said that most Whites who do not identify themselves with an ethnic group think of themselves as "regular Americans." That concept speaks volumes about what it means to be a part of the dominant culture—to be "regular." Therefore, we would be remiss not to include a discussion of Whites in this chapter.

Americans of English ancestry represent about a quarter of the population in the United States, and the dominant American culture is primarily Anglo. The Anglo influence in this country has evolved over the years so that it cannot be truly described as purely White Anglo Saxon Protestant; however, neither is it pluralistic. Characteristics that describe the dominant culture include rugged individualism, task orientation, hard work, success orientation, future orientation, and stoicism. Values attributed to this group include linear problem solving, insight and reason, nuclear family, and Christianity. These characteristics and values still tend to dominate American society. This influence is obvious when one reviews the common U.S. culture experienced by all Americans that is outlined by Axelson (1999). That structure includes (a) a political system that is democratic, requires citizens to obey the laws decided on by the majority, recognizes human equality before the law, freedom of choice, tolerance, and respect for each other's rights; (b) an economic system that emphasizes free enterprise, private ownership, and values diligence, excellence, and respect for economic and professional success; (c) an educational system that provides education for all classes of society and diffuses useful knowledge, tolerance, and character development; and (d) a common language of English, although knowledge of at least one other language is encouraged. When authors speak of the American culture or of the dominant White culture, they are referring to this structure.

Whites are often referred to in the multicultural literature as if they were one homogeneous group. As we study ethnic groups, racial groups, and subcultures, it would be appalling to think that any group is homogeneous. In fact, McGoldrick et al. (1996) broke down White Americans into the following groups: Amish, English ancestry, Dutch, French Canadian, German, Greek, Hungarian, Irish, Italian, Portuguese, and Scandinavian. In addition, there are chapters on Jewish families (which may or may not be White) and Slavic families. Interestingly, Whites from identifiable ethnic origins often differ from Anglo culture as much as non-Whites. For example, the extended family is as important as the nuclear family among Greek Americans, Italian Americans, and Jewish Americans. Also, whereas Anglos are stoic, expression of emotion is encouraged in Jewish and Italian families. Interdependence is encouraged and independence (such as moving away from the family) is discouraged. In fact, many members of these White ethnic groups live in close proximity to one another and maintain customs of the "Old Country." Moreover, there are communities that are, for example, primarily Greek, Italian, Polish, and Jewish in large cities across the United States. Many individuals in these communities have chosen not to assimilate into the dominant "Anglo" culture. Counselors, therefore, are required to have as much sensitivity and knowledge of the cultural differences in these groups as they need to work with ethnic minorities.

As regards education and career development, White ethnic groups also have unique concerns. Among Greek and Italian Americans, for example, higher education is less important than are moral education and family. In fact, it is the family focus that provides the impetus for family-owned businesses that are common in these ethnic groups. Jewish families, in contrast, value higher education and professional achievement highly. Whether or not there may be a historical basis for them, there continue to be career stereotypes for different White ethnic groups, for example, Irish police officers, Italian mafia, Jewish bankers, or Greek restaurateurs. Finally, to think that all White Americans are part of the middle and upper classes is to neglect the largest group of poor people in the Unites States—White Americans. Unfortunately, there is a culture of poverty in the United States that tends to transcend race and ethnicity. Counselors need to be aware of these issues when working with clients on career and family concerns.

❧ Career Counseling and Families ❧

In recent years, there has been some work in the career literature on attachment theory that is relevant to the connection of family and career issues. Ketterson and Bluestein (1997) outlined the application of attachment theory to career exploration, and since then Bluestein (Bluestein et al., 2001; Schultheiss & Bluestein, 1994) and others (Schultheiss & Flum, 2001; Schultheiss, Kress, Manzi, & Glasscock, 2001) have begun the empirical exploration of the interface between work and interpersonal relationships. In this work, they have found that both culture and social class affect interpersonal and work relationships. In addition, Schultheiss et al. (2001) found that not only are parents important in the career decision-making process of young adults, but siblings and other relatives also can be equally as important for security and support. Schultheiss et al. stated, "these relationships may be particularly important within racial/ethnic groups valuing collectivism" (p. 221).

Zunker (1998) observed that problems from work might spill over into a person's family life just as conflicts at home can influence a person's performance at work. As the dual-career/dual-earner trend increases and as more and more individuals become involved in working at home, the line between family life and work will become even thinner. As such, it is imperative that counselors who work with families are able to help them prepare for a lifestyle that includes career as a major component for all members, from the youngest child to the oldest adult in the family. Assuming that career development occurs throughout the life span, then career counseling needs to start when the child is very young, even before he or she enters school. Sometimes parents, particularly ethnic minority parents, feel limited in the kind of help they can give their children because (a) they may be unclear about their role, (b) they may be overstressed by providing for the family with multiple jobs, or (c) they may have so many other issues that they just do not have the energy to help out their children in this area (Herr & Cramer, 1996). By understanding these multiple career issues, therapists in every setting can help families with career development for all family members. In the example cited at the beginning of this chapter, and others presented in later chapters, many of these barriers can be observed.

Most of the literature on career counseling and families addresses the issue of dual-career or dual-earner families. In dual-earner families, both spouses work but at least one of them is working to supplement the family income and not toward building a career future. In dual-career families, both spouses are equally involved in a career (usually professionals) following a particular career ladder. In ethnic minority households, it is typical for both spouses to work because it is often an economic necessity, and they may be dual-earner or dual-career combinations. Again, the scenario above reinforces this condition. For some ethnic groups with this arrangement, household duties have been restructured so that each spouse has an equal share. For other groups, the fact that the mother has to work is a shameful condemnation of the father's inability to provide for his family. It is important to ascertain the family's cultural reaction to the dual-career or dual-earner status rather than making assumptions based on their membership in any cultural group.

There is little discussion in the literature of the use of family systems theories in multicultural career counseling. However, Sciarra (1999) listed some criticisms that multicultural researchers and experts have made of family systems approaches. Among the criticisms were that the family systems approaches (a) were Eurocentric and based on a White middle-class American concept of a normal family, with other kinds of family structures being considered dysfunctional; (b) ignored the fact that there are, in general, a number of different kinds of family structures other than the nuclear family; (c) failed to adjust the notion as to what is and what is not enmeshment in a family based on cultural norms; and (d) were too narrow and do not consider a wider client base in relation to race, gender, ethnicity, and culture.

Fortunately, recent approaches and innovations in the family coun-seling literature have addressed the multicultural issues cited as the crit-icisms above. In their book *Ethnicity and Family Therapy*, McGoldrick et al. (1996) introduced the reader to the complexities of family life as it is affected by the multiple cultures that compose U.S. society. And oth-ers (Hardy & Laszloffy, 1992; Laszloffy & Hardy, 2000) have opened the family therapy community to research and practice that demonstrates the unique conditions that culture brings to the therapeutic table. One can also reflect on the earlier work of Bronfenbrenner (1977) to evoke the complexities of thriving in a society with so many demands. His emphasis on "nested" structures that include the microsystems, mesosys-tems, exosystems, and macrosystems provides a means for building a framework for understanding the contexts in which families function. In Vontress, Johnson, and Epp's (1999) existential model of nature, one's genetic endowment and life experiences are filtered through five layers, including universal, ecological, national, regional, and racial-ethnic cul-ture, which results in the individual's existence. A study of the develop-mental pathways portrayed by Comer (1988) also provides an avenue for anticipating one's success in life. Too many theories exist to be effec-tively presented in this limited text, and of course it is not the purpose of this book to provide that detail. The reader is encouraged to study these and other models that address the contextual issues confronting families and individuals as they explore their life's work. Given the nature of the hypotheses presented in this book, we felt that one model that lends itself to the complexities of culture, career, and family is *nar-rative family therapy* (White & Epston, 1990). By no means are we implying that other established approaches to family therapy cannot accommodate this holistic approach. As the model is further developed in chapter 2, you will see how the narrative model is used in working with families. This constuctivist (Patton & McMahon, 1999; Sexton, 1997) approach to having families tell their story allows the therapist to understand how clients pull from their culture and family histories to make effective career decisions.

୨ Summary ଏ

Career development is a significant factor in the healthy emergence of the individual. As individual career development is enhanced, so goes the evolution of the family in which the individual belongs. Family ther-apists must consider the role that career plays in family life and deter-mine the impact that each family member's career development has on the functioning of the family. Furthermore, and perhaps more inclusive, the therapist needs to consider the complexities involved when intro-ducing culture and ethnicity to the formula. Choosing a career is but the end result of a dynamic process of self-awareness, exploration, planning, and decision making. This process can only be effective when cultural, ethnic, and familial themes are addressed. As Bluestein stated in the January 2001 issue of *The Counseling Psychologist* devoted to work and relationships, counselors "will need to develop a metaperspective that facilitates the ability to maintain an unbiased and affirming focus on multiple contextual domains simultaneously" (p.186). In the next chapter, we offer our ideas on how we can accomplish this task.

၆ References ၆

Arredondo, P.,Toporek, R., Brown, S. P.,Jones,J., Locke, D. C., Sanchez,J., & Stadler, H. (1996). Operationalization of the multicultural counseling competencies. *Journal of Multicultural Counseling and Development, 24,* 42-78.

Axelson, J.A. (1999). *Counseling and development in a multicultural society.* Pacific Grove, CA: Brooks/Cole.

Bluestein, D. (2001).The influence of work and relationships: Critical knowledge for 21st century psychology. *The Counseling Psychologist, 29,* 179-192.

Bluestein, D., Fama, L., Finkelberg, S., Ketterson,T., Schaefer, B., Schwam, M., Sirin, S., & Skau, M. (2001). A qualitative analysis of counseling case material: Listening to our clients. *The Counseling Psychologist, 29,* 240-258.

Bronfenbrenner, U. (1977).Toward an experimental ecology of human development. *American Psychologist, 32,* 513-531.

Carter, E., & McGoldrick, M. (Eds.). (1988). *The changing family life cycle: A framework for family therapy* (2nd ed.). Boston:Allyn & Bacon.

Comer, J. (1988, November). Educating poor and minority children. *Scientific American,* 42-48.

Friesen, J. (1986). The role of the family in vocational development. *International Journal for the Advancement of Counseling, 9,* 5-10.

Gottfredson, L. S. (1981). Circumscription and compromise: A developmental theory of occupational aspirations. *Journal of Counseling Psychology, 26,* 545-579.

Gysbers, N. C., Heppner, M. J., & Johnston, J. A., (1998). *Career counseling: Process, issues, and techniques.* Boston:Allyn & Bacon.

Hardy, K.V., & Laszloffy,T.A. (1992).Training racially sensitive family therapists: Context, content, and contact. *Families in Society: The Journal of Contemporary Human Services, 73,* 364-370.

Herr, E. L., & Cramer, S. H. (1996). *Career guidance and counseling through the life span: Systematic approaches* (5th ed.). New York: HarperCollins.

Herring, R. D. (1998). *Career counseling in schools: Multicultural and developmental perspectives.* Alexandria,VA:American Counseling Association.

Hotchkiss, L., & Borow, H. (1990). Sociological perspectives on work and career development. In D. Brown & L. Brooks (Eds.), *Career choice and development:Applying contemporary theories to practice* (2nd ed.). San Francisco: Jossey-Bass.

Ketterson,T., & Bluestein, D. (1997). Attachment relationships and the career exploration process. *Career Development Quarterly, 46,* 167-178.

Kinnier, R. T., Brigman, S. L., & Noble, F. C. (1990). Career indecision and family enmeshment. *Journal of Counseling and Development, 68,* 309-312.

Krumboltz, J. D. (1994). Improving career development theory from a social learning perspective. In M. L. Savikas & R. W. Lent (Eds.), *Convergence in career development theories: Implications for science and practice* (pp. 9-31). Palo Alto, CA: Consulting Psychologists Press.

Laszloffy, T. A., & Hardy, K. V. (2000). Uncommon strategies for a common problem: Addressing racism in family therapy. *Family Process, 39,* 35-50.

Lee, W. M. L. (1999). *An introduction to multicultural counseling.* Philadelphia: Accelerated Development.

McGoldrick, M., & Giordano, J. (1996). Overview: Ethnicity and family therapy. In M. McGoldrick, J. Giordano, & J. K. Pearce (Eds.), *Ethnicity and family therapy* (2nd ed., pp. 1-27). New York: Guilford Press.

McGoldrick, M., Giordano, J., & Pearce, J. K. (Eds.). (1996). *Ethnicity and family therapy* (2nd ed.). New York: Guilford Press.

Paniagua, F. A. (1996). Cross-cultural guidelines in family therapy practice. *The Family Journal: Counseling and Therapy for Couples and Families, 4,* 127-138.

Patton, W., & McMahon, M. (1999). *Career development and systems theory.* Pacific Grove, CA: Brooks/Cole.

Peterson, N., & Gonzalez, R. C. (2000). *The role of work in people's lives: Applied career counseling and vocational psychology.* Belmont, CA: Brooks/Cole.

Rockwell, T. (1987). The social construction of careers: Career development and career counseling viewed from a sociometric perspective. *Journal of Group Psychotherapy, Psychodrama and Sociometry, 1,* 93-107.

Rotter, J. C., & Hawley, L. D. (1998). Therapeutic approaches with immigrant families. *The Family Journal: Counseling and Therapy for Couples and Families, 6,* 219-222.

Rowland, D. T. (1991). Family diversity and the life cycle. *Journal of Comparative Family Studies, 22,* 1-14.

Schultheiss, D., & Bluestein, D. (1994). Role of adolescent-parent relationships in college student development and adjustment. *Journal of Counseling Psychology, 41,* 248-255.

Schultheiss, D., & Flum, H. (2001). Dialogues and challenges: The interface between work and relationships in transition. *Counseling Psychologist, 29,* 250-270.

Schultheiss, D., Kress, H., Manzi, A., & Glasscock, J. (2001). Relational influences in career development: A qualitative inquiry. *Counseling Psychologist, 29,* 214-239.

Sciarra, D. T. (1999). *Multiculturalism in counseling.* Itasca, IL: Peacock.

Sexton, T. L. (1997). Constructivist thinking within the history of ideas: The challenge of a new paradigm. In T. L. Sexton & B. L. Griffin (Eds.), *Constructivist thinking in Counseling practice, research, and training* (pp. 13-18). New York: Teachers College Press.

Sharf, R. S. (1997). *Applying career development theory to counseling.* Belmont, CA: Brooks/Cole.

Super, D. E. (1985). Career counseling across cultures. In P. Pederson (Ed.), *Handbook of cross-cultural counseling and therapy* (pp. 11–20). Westport, CT: Greenwood Press.

Vontress, C. E., Johnson, J. A., & Epp, L. R. (1999). *Cross-cultural counseling: A Casebook*. Alexandria, VA: American Counseling Association.

Weinger, S. (1998). Children living in poverty: Their perception of career opportunities. *Families in Society: The Journal of Contemporary Human Service, 79*, 320–330.

White, M., & Epston, D. (1990). *Narrative means to therapeutic ends*. New York: Norton.

Zunker, V. G. (1998). *Career counseling: Applied concepts of life planning* (5th ed.). Pacific Grove, CA: Brooks/Cole.

Part II

☙

Theoretical Perspectives

Chapter 2

Out of the Box:
A Model for Counseling in the
Twenty-First Century

Joshua M. Gold, Joseph C. Rotter, and Kathy M. Evans

This chapter describes the rationale and proposed modality designed to encourage counselors to experiment with "moving out of the box." By labeling it "moving out of the box," we intend to ask counselors to question their current counseling modalities and to consider the model explained in this chapter and exemplified through the case studies presented in this book. The challenge we as counselors face is how to extend the ways in which we conceptualize client issues, how we intervene with client presenting concerns, or a combination of both agendas. At this stage of the evolution of counseling approaches, we believe that the next progression of theory and practice involves an integration of models whose integration may have been overlooked. So the objective of this chapter is less to present new information to counselors than to offer a new way, perhaps, to think about what is already known.

This chapter's objective revolves around the presentation of a *practice model* rather than a theory of counseling. A practice model emphasizes new ways of thinking about clients as a vehicle toward new intervention orientations, whereas a counseling theory grapples with questions regarding human nature, the etiology of client dysfunction, and counseling goals, as well as proposing interventions congruent with the tenets of that specific theory. In addition to this distinction, as the proposed orientation integrates career, multicultural, and family approaches, a familiarity with the most current and research-supported models from each genre is a vital prerequisite for making full use of this synthesis.

Part of the question that arises with any proposed model of counseling is the extent to which the suggested model offers "add-on" techniques and the extent to which the new modality requires a shift in counselor orientation. These two dimensions are not exclusive. One can add techniques to one's therapeutic repertoire without changing a clinical worldview in any appreciable fashion. For example, a cognitive–behavioral counselor could integrate a technique such as reframing without having to recreate his or her style of case conceptualization. In that instance, the new technique would be congruent with the existing process of case conceptualization. However, a counselor cannot evaluate or refine a world perspective without then contemplating which techniques currently in one's therapeutic "toolbox" remain congruent with one's emerging epistemology. We assume that counseling interventions need to follow one's conceptual model to provide counselors, and clients, with a consistent theme of thought and intervention. For example, if that same counselor decided to focus more on the behavioral counseling model than the cognitive aspects by emphasizing observable client action and the response of the client's environment to those behavior changes, then the reframing techniques would become incongruent with the emerging counseling orientation. The counselor would be faced with the incongruence between case conceptualization (behavior change as an intended outcome) and technique (cognitive insight, evaluation, and possible change as a method toward that intended objective of client change).

The title of this chapter highlights our admonition for counselors to begin to consider an epistemological evolution and offers two complex considerations for clinicians: (a) In what boxes do we find ourselves, and what are the advantages and limitations of such positions? and (b) How does the birth of a new century, and millennium, offer opportunities for professional self-redefinition?

As counselors, we have each developed a specific clinical epistemology or worldview. While we acknowledge our ongoing responsibility to attend to the welfare of our clients by the most proven means available, it is easy to become so busy with our professional routine that we do not commit the time to consider the next evolution in our professional orientations. We may ask the question "What could I do with this client?" in search for new interventions, but we may overlook the more complex question, "How can I think about my client in new ways that may be more inclusive or descriptive of the client's world?" As explained previously, the first question is not inherently faulty. It is, however, inherently limiting because its answer tends to expand one's clinical skill array but only to the limits of one's clinical epistemology. A statement such as "That may work for you, but I can't see myself integrating it into my practice" exemplifies an epistemological boundary issue. In this case, the difficulty is less the counselor's ability to understand or practice the suggested intervention than the counselor's inability or reluctance to examine his or her clinical belief system about clients, counseling, and the counselor's role. It is the second question that fosters epistemological "wondering."

An epistemology is defined as a "branch of philosophy that investigates the origin, nature, methods and limits of human knowledge" (Gladding, Remley, & Huber, 2001, p. 234). As counselors, we each develop an idiosyncratic epistemology, a personal amalgam of counseling theory tempered by clinical and life experiences, that we apply to organize and explain our lives and the experiences of our clients. Our epistemology directs our decisions regarding case conceptualizations, portends our choices of interventions, and mandates our definitions of success in counseling. It is our ongoing successful practice within such a framework that confirms our professional identity and our suitability for this profession and enhances our professional self-esteem. However, such a perspective can seem seductive by suggesting that there are no other, equally valid, views of the same issue.

Therefore, the attitudes that confirm us professionally may also limit us professionally. As the professional literature reports new developments in theory and outcome studies, we are constantly challenged to evaluate our models of practice in light of these findings. Although the "box" offers comfort, security, and predictability, it may trap us into the delusion that we do not need to continue to evolve with our profession. However, we believe that as counselors, we all have a professional responsibility to grow—a process that we know perhaps better than anyone to be challenging, upsetting, perhaps threatening, but an ongoing life task for us to recognize and make full use of our as-of-yet hidden talents.

The goal of the proposed model is to provide a framework for counselors engaged in career counseling that will be inclusive of the multiple issues that direct and affect a client's life. In the process of conceptualizing a model that integrates culture, family, and career, it became clear that career decision making and satisfaction were the dependent variables. Although career issues may affect the family and culture, we assert that the influences of family and culture affect the career development of individuals to a far greater extent than career choices affect family and culture. It is for that reason that we have singled out career and lifestyle as the primary focus of this integrative model. However, the model is deliberately designed to draw in counselors from all specialty areas.

୨ Getting Out of the Box ୧

Often the existence of specialty areas in counseling promotes the notion that there is no overlap in the epistemology, conceptualization process, and needed interventions, with a resulting temptation to "box oneself" into one of those areas. It is easy to see oneself as a career counselor, or substance abuse counselor, or student affairs specialist, or family counselor. Although such a declaration of emphasis does narrow one's professional focuses and allows one to concentrate professional energies into an area of specialization, it may serve to exclude or limit other ways of thinking, as the connection between what is offered as new and what has been tried and proven effective may not be readily apparent. Part of our ongoing mandate is not to ask whether connections exist but to investigate how these two ideas can connect. It is that shift in orientation that fosters a holistic or inclusive, rather than a reductionist, view. We ask counselors to reflect on their needs to balance professional security with ongoing professional growth. We encourage all counselors to get out of their respective boxes (specialty areas such as career counseling or family counseling) and to reach out to clients in areas that might be less familiar to them professionally but that have a substantial influence on a client's life.

Figure 2.1 is a graphic representation of getting out of the box. It shows that when counselors turn themselves around, different perspectives can pop out, like a jack-in-the-box. Marriage and family counselors suddenly see career and multicultural issues with equal importance, and multicultural counselors see marriage and family and career concerns as equally valid.

Traditionally, individuals who are engaged in family counseling and personal counseling or psychotherapy did not address (to any significant degree) a client's career issues. Even though separating the personal and career concerns of a client has been discouraged for decades, and even though almost *all* counselors have been trained in career development, career counseling has become a counseling specialty area, leading other counselors to believe that career counseling is not their job. This is an unfortunate belief, because all clients of all counselors have careers. The U.S. society is changing, client problems are changing, and counseling needs to keep changing as well. Some of the

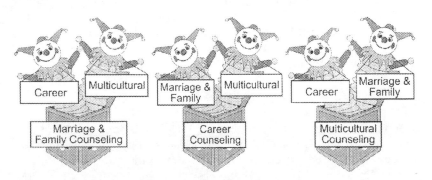

Figure 2.1. Getting out of the box.

greatest changes in counseling in the 21st century may involve clients' career concerns.

❧ Emergence of Career Counseling ❧

Most of social history has been characterized by the assumption that career "aspiration" is a function of birth and social position rather than aptitude and interest. Children were expected to follow in parental career "footsteps": Their choices were virtually nonexistent. However, the notion of career choice evolved with the Renaissance and became, over time, an integral thread of the American social fabric. Career counseling was initiated in a social climate that stressed rugged individualism and advocated "pulling oneself up by one's bootstraps" to "become one's own man." Implicit in those directives are the assumptions that a career is one, and perhaps the most important, vehicle of self-definition for a contributing individual in 20th-century society. Admired were the virtues of competition, self-imitation, sacrifice, and accomplishment, accompanied by a view of the heroic individual caring for self at the expense of all others (McAuliffe & Eriksen, 1999). In summary, the notion of being a successful career person equated to those notions of the "superior" masculine identity.

However, during the latter years of the 20th century, these definitions have come under scrutiny and eventually criticism. It is from this scrutiny that the theory, and practice, of career development began to undergo the difficult process of integrating relational and sociological components into the established individualistic aspects. Again, this view serves as a process of integration rather than omission. Career counselors still consider a client's interest, aptitudes, and skills as crucial insights for satisfying career decision making. However, these individual insights, regardless of how illuminating, are insufficient for truly "informed" career decision making. The notion that individuals make career decisions in a social vacuum has been questioned.

❧ A Social Constructivist Perspective ❧

As individuals, we all are influenced by and, recursively, impact our families and communities. We are not as "individual" as we may think or even hope, but rather present for counseling as a representative, or reflection, of our relational and sociological contexts. What we have learned about ourselves as a family member, son or daughter, male or female, member of a specific religious group, racial or ethnic group, and so on are vital components of our self-definition, in our career concerns as well as general life decisions. We can no more separate ourselves from these influences than we could change our past, because we bring the sum total of our life experiences, viewing through and being viewed through those relational and sociological lens, to counseling. When counselors omit contextual factors in any type of counseling, the client is ill equipped to return to his or her family and community with change in mind. In fact, that omission may ill prepare the client for the unfavorable welcome he or she may receive from his or her social system, as the individual decision may be seen contrary to the social view and may serve to isolate the individual from the very social system whose support is so desired at this time of challenge and exploration. A synopsis of previous research (see Fox & Bartholomae, 2000) substantiates the impacts of career decisions on individuals, couples, and families across all studied cultural groups.

Although clients have internalized many of those overt and tacit messages from culture and family and could claim their ownership, they cannot claim their authorship. Rather, it is the mandates of society, filtered through culture, adopted by one's family, and prescribed into gender roles that have contributed to the "social" aspects of the client's presenting problem (Wilkinson, 1999). These imposed roles serve a homeostatic function for any social group, maintaining and solidifying roles and expectations. However, these definitions can also play a restrictive role. These implicit social mandates also limit or define the amount of change one can make in one's life and still expect to be accepted by one's social systems. Therefore, for each person, a tension exists within this viewpoint: how much of "me" must I sacrifice to be accepted by those close to me versus how much of who I aspire to be can be expressed and yet accommodated within my social and cultural networks. The task of the career counselor within this framework is to help the individual recognize the power of this dilemma and to seek answers that will serve clients in both individual and relational contexts.

As counselors get out of their respective boxes and develop a holistic or multifaceted approach to working with clients with career concerns, they will be much better prepared to integrate the cultural, social, and career questions that provide a contextual foundation for understanding the client's unique view of his or her own world. Looking head in the new century, and at the need for counseling to change, four related areas of concern are apparent:

1. In the early 21st century, what are society's mandates about career, culture, and family?
2. How have differing cultures interpreted those societal injunctions?
3. How do theories of family development and career development overlap?
4. How do gender roles influence career development?

This model advocates a postmodern or social constructivist epistemology. Again, by epistemology, we are referring to the process by which we make sense of our world, in addition to the sense we make. There are many options by which one can perceive one's world. For example, a scientific model would deal with only observable, measurable properties and may translate into a behavioral orientation to the world, believing that feelings and thoughts cannot be directly perceived but only inferred by observed action. Nihilism, as a belief system, advocates a lack of meaning in one's existence, that one's life is merely random events lacking purpose or direction. Whichever belief system people adopt, and it is impossible to function without such a guiding belief system, its tenets direct how people make life choices and how they understand the choices that others make.

From a social constructivist perspective, we believe that individuals each create a unique picture of the world and a unique explanation for how their lives have unfolded. That view of their lives, subjective reality, or personal interpretation of their experience of the world is either confirmed or amended through interaction with significant others (Andrews & Clark, 1998; Cottone, 2001; McAuliffe & Eriksen, 1999). From birth, people's interactions with family members and significant others shape their views of the world. For example, if I come from a family in which formal education is prized, I would integrate a perception that doing well in school is an important part of my self-definition and is a vital means by which I receive validation from my family members and social community. I may even disparage peers who do not hold the same belief by saying, "If they knew what was good for them, they'd study more." I may also have little tolerance for classmates who do not put the same emphasis on academic success as I do, and I would be consistently puzzled by peers whose post–high school plans did not include higher education. However, from a social constructive viewpoint, their beliefs, while foreign to mine, do reflect the same process of intrafamilial formulation as did mine, but with decidedly different outcomes.

The final product of this interactional process becomes, for lack of a better term, one's personal "truth." For the purposes of this discussion, *truth* is defined as the way in which each person creates, organizes, and gives meaning to life events. That contrived meaning contributes to one's notion of "reality" (Pakman, 1999)—one's particular idea of how the world does, and should, operate. However, in addition to one's personal interpretation of an event, that version remains open to confirmation or negation by the significant others in one's lives (Etchison & Kleist, 2000). This tacit "negotiation of truth" evolves into a chronology of events, or recounting of how one came to be as one currently is, that both an individual and the important others in his or her social world can accept. Family and cultural stories provide the "building blocks" of a person's worldview. Family and cultural approval become the "mortar" that binds these blocks together into a unified whole. Within family and culture, this shared epistemology offers a sense of security and predictability for how an individual and others in his or her world make sense of life events. Without such a structure, regardless of its specific content, the world would seem chaotic and frightening.

This understanding of one's life stories is composed of three related constructs. First, what are the sources of understanding of one's world? Second, how does one organize one's life experiences in light of social and cultural influences? Third, what meaning and organization has one created and how does that schema serve the individual in his or her social systems?

Such a stance is predicated on an emerging assumption of personal ownership for one's worldview. One can look to the impact of one's family, and other cultural factors in the crystallization of one's worldview (Killian, 2001; Pakman, 1999), as insight. Restricting one's present or future life choices based on one's family history or culture or specific gender becomes a fruitless waste of energy for two vital reasons. First, as individuals, we cannot change those aspects of our past; and, second, by inflating how our historical factors impede our lives, we overlook the strengths and assets that our stories describing our place in those systems uncover. Perhaps, in this case, the most harmful story that we tell ourselves is that being "___" (who we are) has no positive qualities, no strengths, and no sense of legacy of which one can feel proud and on which one can build.

❧ Family Life Stories ☙

It is important, as individuals, to begin the search for the origins of our worldviews and to acknowledge that the stories that define us reflect the unique familial and cultural connections of our past. One should not blame one's culture or family for the creation and transmission of certain life views. At the time of their origin, those stories made perfect sense to their authors and served a vital sustaining function within their social system. The task is to honor the efforts made to explain life and the world and to understand how vital such stories are to the history and coherence of one's family and community. Although those stories may seem outmoded or constricting at the present time or in one's current situation, at the time of their creation, those explanations were the best the family and culture could produce.

Family and cultural socialization processes imprint on individuals the stories and assumptions propagandized by families and larger social networks to explain the common social reality (McAuliffee & Eriksen,

1999; Minuchin, 1998). Growing up in one's own family and hearing the same explanations over and over again, it is easy to see how one could come to accept them as a given or a fact. Children are expected to assimilate these stories completely, and do so for three vital reasons. First, in most families and cultures, there are emotional penalties as a result of questioning or refusing to accept these stories (Rockwell, 1987). Children risk scorn, derision, and the fear of emotional isolation as a consequence of challenging existing views. Second, given a limited world experience, children cannot be expected to offer competing views that would fit the family equally well. Third, the family elders have a vested interest in the propagation of these stories, as their sense of self-definition is rooted in those views.

Whatever sense of comfort and security these stories offer to children, and however strongly these threads bind family and culture, individuals do have a right to begin to question the relevance to their current life situations. Their life-long adoption reflects a narrow view of self, usually predominated by emphasis on perceived individual weakness (Schwartz, 1999). This blind adherence to cultural and family stories reflects emotional foreclosure on the part of the individual rather than individual understanding and purposeful choice. Emotional foreclosure implies a hasty acceptance because the explanation is readily available and widely accepted, not because the explanation makes particular sense or fits one's life situation. In addition, accepting popular lore ensures that one's acceptance within one's family and culture is not threatened by the risk of espousing a differing but perhaps more individually meaningful view.

Within the proposed framework, one's career "story," with all its attendant beliefs, injunctions, and mythologies, becomes open to retelling. However, in this oration, the messages are examined for their current contribution to career direction, beliefs, aspirations, and so on, and the author is legitimized in choosing to retain or "edit" his or her story (Etchison & Kleist, 2000; Schwartz, 1999). Based on personal relevance as balancing a cultural or family sense of obligation with one's career aspirations, one's career themes become evaluated as a celebration of personal strengths, talents, and aptitudes. For example, one may discover that the family legacy of not pursuing postsecondary education and being proud of one's position as a manual worker had less to do with a lack of individual talents and rather reflects a common Depression-era justification for a lack of sufficient family funds to support college dreams. In this instance, the story served a mollifying effect of helping family members to resign themselves to a financial reality that may no longer exist.

Therefore, as counselors, we advocate that one's truth may be seen as forever fluid, always open for redefinition (Killian, 2001; McAuliffe &

Eriksen, 1999). However, this opportunity for redefinition can only exist when one accepts the notions that one's truth merely reflects those aspects of social desirability that one has chosen to adopt. The process of choice and invention of new truths must serve two agendas. First, these new truths must assist the individual in defining and moving toward a career dream unique to the individual. Second, these new stories must also serve to enhance one's connections with one's social support systems and meaningful relationships. Specific to this work, it is not only the differing aspects of family and cultural influences on career development but also the personal interaction between those influences that dictate the eventual career self-definitions.

From conceptual and interventional perspectives, career counseling then becomes a reflection of narrative approaches to helping. Narrative therapies revolve around the stories that people tell to explain their lives (Goldenberg & Goldenberg, 2000). Although those stories may seem to describe people, places, and events, a reflection on their emerging themes offers insight into how each individual integrates the personally heard dictates of culture and family into life career themes. These stories reveal people's selected knowledge about themselves, about the symbols or meanings that they value (Patton & McMahon, 1999), and about the world with which they choose to surround themselves. Over time, people create such stories to "make sense" of their lives and begin to accept those stories as not only true of their past but also a basis for interpretation of subsequent experiences. However, often the stories include messages of control or morality as espoused by the dominant culture (Fredman & Combs, 1996, as cited by Minuchin, 1998), which serve not to empower the individual but rather to limit life, choices (White, 1997).

Therefore, stories are to be examined through a cultural "lens," focusing on what their adoption says about one's integration of dominant and minority culture values, and how this integration serves to support, or demean, one's cultural identity for the sake of social conformity. As a process of finding a "truer" career, and life direction, one begins to reconnect with one's true career dreams, values, beliefs, and commitments. Part of the process of reexamination involves the reduction in the emotional investment one holds in the specific story to be replaced with an acknowledgment that the guiding themes may be maintained, may be discarded, may be "edited," or may be shelved as an old favorite book whose story one has transcended but whose ongoing presence provides a sense of history and reassurance.

Through questioning assigned meanings and interpretations, the client begins to distinguish between event and experience (Gladding, 1998). While the event itself is objective (either this or that happened or did not happen), the client's unique experience of that event has fashioned his or her truth about the event but also serves as a blueprint by which the client interprets future-like events (Goldenberg & Goldenberg, 2000). This repetition of stories and generalization of these "myths" to new situations anchors the distortive lens in one's personal mythology, thereby extending power to control one's life interpretations. The vehicle for change is then twofold: (a) to detach from a storyline that has dominated one's thinking but produced unwanted results and (b) to begin to create an alternative account of oneself (Gladding, 1998).

This approach contradicts sharply with traditional scientific thought that an objective truth exists separate from the individual and can somehow be "discovered." From that stance, one is expected to "own" a "truth" that one has had no input in shaping. However, an individual is expected to believe that others, those external "truth makers," know better than the individual what will be in his or her best career interests. Implicit within this assumption is a dangerous double-bind: that conformity is the path to individual career satisfaction and the more widespread the consensus of career choice and aspiration, the more correct it must be. Within that "logico-scientific" reasoning, characterized by empiricism and the illusion of rational thought (Gladding, 1998), problems are seen to reside within individuals and conform to an external code of diagnostic criteria in order to be truly problematic. What is, and is not, appropriate for the individual is then decided by others irrespective of that person. One set of societal standards is then imposed with an expectation that these definitions will become internalized, and the sanction for nonconformity becomes punishment or exclusion. This notion of "one grand narrative" applicable to all (Savickas, 1993, p. 211) is no longer feasible, if it ever once was.

᭥ Out-of-the-Box Model ᭢

Given the complexities of family, culture, and career briefly outlined in this chapter, one quickly discovers that the infinite number of combinations of characteristics makes it impossible to establish a "cookie cutter" model for counseling. Even when career or lifestyle development is used as the dependent variable, the familial and cultural influences on this development become exceedingly complex to explain in generalities. However, to simplify the process by controlling for these significant influences does little justice to the process. Perhaps the contribution of this model lies less in the answers it provides than in the admonition for a different type of questioning by the counselor, directing the client to explore what may have previously been seen as unrelated aspects of himself or herself.

Consequently, the model that follows (see Figure 2.2) offers not a template for lifestyle planning and career development but uses an hourglass conceptualization, whereby the variables related to culture, family, and society are combined with individual characteristics such as interests, aptitudes, and education that are siphoned through each individual and translated into idiosyncratic epistemologies—an individual's lifestyle evolution or lifestyle focal point. In turn, this lifestyle selection opens opportunities for the individual that consequently affects culture and family. As one then reverses the hourglass, the mix again reaches a focal point, which represents another developmental point in one's career evolution.

The hourglass is a graphic representation of the *out-of-the-box model* for combining culture, family, and career issues in counseling. The upper portion of the hourglass accepts the array of cultural, familial, and career phenomena that the client brings to counseling. The narrowed portion of the hourglass symbolizes the union of these phenomena and is the lifestyle focal point. At this point, the union of these phenomena

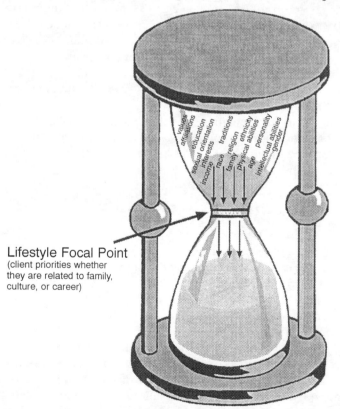

Lifestyle Focal Point
(client priorities whether
they are related to family,
culture, or career)

Figure 2.2. Out-of-the-Box model.

forces an interaction that creates a new construct in the lower portion of the hourglass. As the hourglass is turned, the mix again is forced through the narrow opening resulting in yet another mix. This process is repeated throughout one's career life with different constructs resulting from the ever-changing mix. Thus, as these new paradigms are formed through changing family constellation, career development, and cultural adaptation to change, so too is the portrayal of counseling.

The proposed model is a practice model as opposed to a theoretical one, designed to assist counselors in seeing client issues from multiple perspectives and intervening with issues that are most important to the client rather than depending on the counselor's own theoretical orientation to define the problem. However individual authors within this book have elected to approach the case examples from their own theoretical frames of reference, their contributions also reflect an adherence to the prescribed model.

To describe the model more concretely, we propose a process whereby the counselor needs to ask the following questions:

1. How well do I understand the client's worldview?
   a. Counselors must assess client problems from multiple perspectives, giving each factor (e.g., all the factors in the top part of the hourglass) equal attention.
   b. Counselors need to listen for client priorities with an open mind and resist the temptation to retreat back into the "box."
   c. As a result of a and b above, the counselor becomes aware of the client's present lifestyle focal point or lifestyle evolution (the smallest part of the hour glass).
2. How are my own cultural values and biases affecting my approach to this client?
   a. Counselors realize that the same factors (in the hourglass) that affect the lifestyle evolution of a client influence their own lifestyle evolution but perhaps to a different degree or in a different manner.
   b. Counselors should be intimately familiar with their own worldviews, values, and biases and aware of how those views could affect a client.
3. Are the interventions I use helpful to my client?
   a. Given the client's lifestyle focal point, the counselors develop interventions that reflect client need.
   b. Counselors easily move into the sphere of counseling that best fits client needs (family counselors may focus on career issues; career counselors may focus on family issues, etc.).
   c. Counselors preferences for working on family, multicultural, or career issues are subordinated by client priorities.

The approach emphasized in the model is intended to provide the counselor with a more comprehensive understanding of the client. Although the model offers an opportunity to be inclusive, there is no guarantee that all significant aspects of the individual will surface. However, as the client shares his or her story, the counselor will better grasp the important parts of the client's world.

❧ Summary ❦

This chapter has offered a rationale for integrating one's professional knowledge of multicultural and family approaches into one's career counseling. By acknowledging the relational and sociological contexts that nurture our career clients, we as counselors are better equipped to help clients consider those factors in their career decision making.

❧ References ❦

Andrews, J., & Clark, D. J. (1998). Postmodern ideas and relational conversations in clinical practice. *The Family Journal, 6,* 316-322.

Cottone, R. R. (2001). A social constructivism model of ethical decision making in counseling. *Journal of Counseling and Development, 79,* 39-45.

Etchison, M., & Kleist, D. M. (2000). Review of narrative therapy: Research and utility. *The Family Journal, 8,* 61-66.

Fox, J. J., & Bartholomae, S. (2000). Economic stress and families. In P. C. McKenry & S. J. Price (Eds.), *Families and change: Coping with stressful events and transitions* (2nd ed., pp. 250-278). Thousand Oaks, CA: Sage.

Gladding, S. T. (1998). *Family therapy: History, theory and practice* (2nd ed.). Upper Saddle River, NJ: Prentice Hall.

Gladding, S. T., Remley, T. P., Jr., & Huber, C. H. (2001). *Ethical, legal, and professional issues in the practice of marriage and family therapy* (3rd ed.). Upper Saddle River, NJ: Prentice Hall.

Goldenberg, I., & Goldenberg, H. (2000). *Family therapy: An overview* (5th ed.). Belmont, CA: Wadsworth.

Killian, K. D. (2001). Reconstituting racial histories and identities: The narratives of interracial couples. *Journal of Marital and Family Therapy, 27,* 27-42.

McAuliffe, G. J., & Eriksen, K. P. (1999). Toward a constructivist and developmental identity for the counseling profession: The context-phase-stage-style model. *Journal of Counseling and Development, 79,* 39-45.

Minuchin, S. (1998). Where is the family in narrative family therapy? *Journal of Marital and Family Therapy, 24,* 397-403.

Pakman, M. (1999). Designing constructive therapies in community mental health: Poetics and micropolitics in and beyond the consulting room. *Journal of Marital and Family Therapy, 25,* 83-98.

Patton, W., & McMahon, M. (1999). *Career development and systems theory: A new relationship.* Pacific Grove, CA: Brooks/Cole.

Rockwell, T. (1987). The social construction of careers: Career development and career counseling viewed from a sociometric perspective. *Journal of Group Psychotherapy, Psychodrama, and Sociometry, 1*, 93–107.

Savickas, M. L. (1993). Career counseling in the postmodern era. *Journal of Cognitive Psychotherapy: An International Quarterly, 7*, 205–215.

Schwartz, R. C. (1999). Narrative therapy expands and contracts family therapy's horizons. *Journal of Marital and Family Therapy, 25*, 263–267.

White, M. (1997). *Narratives of therapists' lives.* Adelaide, Australia: Dulwich Centre.

Wilkinson, D. (1999). Reframing family ethnicity in America. In H. P. McAdoo (Ed.), *Family ethnicity: Strength in diversity* (2nd ed., pp. 15–62). Thousand Oaks, CA: Sage.

~ Chapter 3 ~

Synthesizing Career and Family Theories: Relevant Issues

Patricia Murray, Laurie Williamson, Kimberly Boudrot, Erika Reents, Tamara Roberts, and Kathy M. Evans

In this chapter, we review several career development and family theories. We focus on the treatment of family, culture, and career in each theory and suggest how each could be adapted to fit the out-of-the-box model. Because testing is an integral part of career counseling, a brief review of multicultural issues in career testing is also given. Career theories are addressed first, followed by theories of family therapy.

~ Career Theories ~

The American culture is characterized by an emphasis on verbal communication; a focus on the individual's needs and goals; rational, logical, linear problem-solving approaches to decision making; adherence to time schedules; an emphasis on long-range goals; and a nondirective approach to counseling (D. W. Sue & Sue, 1990). However, counselors working with clients from other cultures must consider other cultural influences in their career development. Therefore, several authors suggest that using a "blanket" format for career counseling is inappropriate (Fouad, 1993; Peterson & Gonzalez, 2000). Lack of consideration of cultures other than the Anglo American culture and the use of inappropriate tools that measure personality and career interests may result in misunderstandings and barriers between counselor and client (Baruth & Manning, 1991; Fouad, 1993; Ibrahim, 1985; D. W. Sue & Sue, 1990; Westermeyer, 1987). The theories of career development have been, in general, less than helpful in assisting counselors to adapt their practice to work with individuals from a wide variety of cultural backgrounds. In addition, most theories do not address, in depth, career issues aside from career decision making.

Vocational choice can arguably be considered one of the most important decisions of a person's life. It is no wonder that much of the literature regarding career theories focuses on career selection more than vocational adjustment. Although career selection is of great importance, a person conceivably spends more time *working in* a specific occupation than in choosing an occupation. In fact, work comprises virtually "two-thirds of the average individual's life and at least one-third of the average adult's day" (Dawis & Lofquist, 1984, p. 7). Given this assertion by Dawis and Lofquist, it is easy to see the importance of work in one's life as well as on one's family. A person's career choice may be influenced by his or her family but that choice also has a great impact on the family.

Multicultural Treatment of Career Theories

It is a fact that the well-known theories of our time have been developed by White, American, middle-class men who live in a mainstream culture. The question remains as to the validity of these theories with populations that differ from the mainstream culture. An individual's culture, gender, ethnic-racial background, language, socioeconomic status, and religious affiliation all affect an individual's personality orientation and environment, thus career options may also be narrowed or expanded.

Clients may have a history in which they have not been afforded the opportunity of experiencing congruence within their careers or have been discouraged in their investigation of alternative career choices (i.e., as a result of racism, sexism, and ageism). If these considerations are not addressed in determining the effectiveness of a theory, then the integrity of that theory may be compromised. The following descriptions offer the differing opinions surrounding the use of career theories to different cultures and races.

Treatment of Family Issues in Career Theories

Just as the theories vary in their approach to multicultural influence, so too are they distinct in their ability to incorporate various family concerns. Specifically, the diverse nature of family systems in the United States is rapidly changing. Changes in the family certainly affect areas outside the family, including career development. The following discussion addresses these concerns as they relate to each theory and its incorporation of family systems.

We believe it is important to review the theories on the basis of how each integrates issues pertaining to multicultural perspectives and family systems. Each theory is rather comprehensive and beyond the scope of this chapter; as a result, we examine an abridged summary of the most salient features. For a more thorough review of the theories, the reader is directed to the following: Dawis (1996), Dawis and Lofquist (1984), Herr (1997), Holland (1992), Krumboltz (1979), Mitchell, Levine, and Krumboltz (1999), Salomone (1996), and Super (1957, 1990).

Donald E. Super

Donald E. Super has greatly influenced career development as he has contributed to the field of careers for over 60 years. His theory of vocational development has survived and prospered, whereas many of the other vocational guidance theories that were introduced from 1951 to 1963 have flourished briefly at best. His career development theory has been known as the "segmented" theory that demonstrates the meaningful relationships between life-span phenomenon and vocational variables (Salomone, 1996). Super proposes that career choices are general statements about the vocational development to people, their characteristics, and their interactions with the work environment. Super explains in one of his early works that the concept of stages provides a foundation for considering a number of vocational issues and problems. Furthermore, Super believes that the life stages construct served as a guiding concept in the planning of educational offerings (Salomone, 1996). Specifically, Super outlines the following vocational life stages model:

Stage I: Growth (birth–14)
> Developmental tasks: when individuals form a picture of themselves and identify with key figures in family, school, and community.

Stage II: Exploration (age 15–24)
> Developmental tasks: when individuals crystallize, specify, and implement occupational choices.

Stage III: Establishment (age 25–44)
> Developmental tasks: when individuals stabilize, consolidate, and advance in their chosen occupation.

Stage IV: Maintenance (age 45–64)
> Developmental tasks: when individuals hold onto, update, and reinvent their chosen occupation.

Stage V: Decline/Disengagement (age 65 on)
> Developmental tasks: when individuals selectively reduce in their pace or workload until they retire.

Super proposes that a person will go through a recycling process in the transition from one stage to the next and may experience "mini-cycles" (new growth, reexamination, and reestablishment) within a stage. Super's perspectives on a life-span, life-space approach to career development evolved as elements leading to such a concept were tested and refined by him and other authors over a 20-year time period.

Super devised a *life-career rainbow model* that portrays different parts of the life span as well as the different roles that a particular individual plays. These roles include child, leisurite, citizen, worker, homemaker, spouse, parent, or pensioner. He used the life-career rainbow model to depict the nature of roles that people play throughout their lives. He explains how these roles emerge, interact, and possibly conflict. Super describes how these roles shape decision points that occur before and at the time of taking on a new role, giving up an old role, and making significant changes in the nature of an existing role (Herr, 1997). In the early 1990s, Super created an archway model to delineate the changing diversity of life roles experienced by individuals over the life span. This model illustrates how biographical, psychological, and socioeconomic determinants influence career development.

Multicultural Issues and Super's Theory. Because career theories were developed by and for European males, the question is, "Can these theories be applied across cultures?" One of the concerns with Super's model has been its lack of extensive consideration of race and ethnicity as factors in career development (Fouad, 1994). One of the great strengths of Super's theory, however, is the flexibility to incorporate cultural variables. In his early writings, Super (1957, 1990) acknowledged the possible influences of race, ethnicity, and socioeconomic status on the processes of career development. Both in the life-career rainbow model and in his archway model (Super, 1990), Super noted that career development emerges from a dynamic interaction between individual factors and socioeconomic and other environmental factors such as school, family, geography, and the labor market (Fouad, 1994). Moreover, he suggested that the socioeconomic–environmental factors may open or close opportunities by shaping occupational concepts and self-concepts.

Career maturity (the ability of an individual to accomplish developmentally appropriate vocational tasks) is a major focus of research regarding the utility of Super's constructs across populations. Several career studies concentrated on career maturity across cultural groups and have found little relationship between career behavior and measures of career maturity (Fouad, 1994). These studies question the construct validity of developmental tasks among non-White ethnic minorities. For example, Rodriquez and Blocher (1988) found that career interventions increased Puerto Rican women's career maturity scores but had little to no effect on the women's decision-making skills. Another study conducted in 1992 found that Black high school youths scored low on career maturity attitudes when compared with norm groups but that attitudes were not significantly related to behaviors considered critical to vocational maturity such as punctuality, responsibility, or attendance (Fouad & Keeley, 1992).

Super was interested in international work, and he spent much time in Britain and France writing about his issues in career counseling across cultures (Super, 1985). He conducted research in Russia, Japan, and Britain; however, he conducted very little research on minority populations in the United States.

The literature reviewed indicates that most of the cross-cultural work on career maturity shows that individuals seem to progress through developmental stages and are accomplishing vocational tasks appropriate to those stages. Current measures of career maturity attitudes, however, seem to lack validity for African Americans, and this points to the need to construct new measures of career maturity that are culturally appropriate. Counselors are being challenged in today's society when addressing the needs of cultures across the board regarding careers and career maturity.

Family Issues and Super's Theory. Super's (1980) life-span, life-space approach advances the notion that the work role is not the only role in which counselors need to attend. He believed that people live in multiple-role environments. In other words, work roles, family roles, educational roles, and community roles vary in their demands on and significance for different individuals and within different developmental periods (Herr, 1997). Career development, according to Super, is viewed as a life-span process consisting of multiple transitions, shifting needs for information, and reassessment of roles and commitments. In addition, this process involves the identification of new questions and dilemmas as these changes occur. Consequently, having an awareness of such transitions allows for a smooth transition in relation to Super's developmental stages throughout the life span.

In addition, Super was one of the first career theorists to outline the career patterns for women (Super, 1957). In this work, Super suggested that there are five career patterns: stable homemaking (never worked), conventional (work until married), double track (homemaking and working), stable working, and unstable (sporadic work pattern). Although his original thesis that women's career patterns are more influenced by family commitments generally still holds, Betz (1984) found that high commitment to a pioneer occupation is no longer unusual for women. In fact, it is more unusual to find the never-worked pattern.

Implications for the Model. Similar to most career development theories, Super's work was originally predicated on the career behavior primarily of White males (Fouad, 1993). However, his theory has since been expanded and applied to many populations and situations beyond original concepts. Much of the cross-cultural work on career maturity shows that individuals progress through developmental stages and are accomplishing vocational tasks appropriate to these stages. The comprehensiveness of the model does allow for easy adaptation to the out-of-the-box model. However, much research needs to be conducted regarding the influences of multicultural, family, and career factors. Counselors have an arduous task at hand when providing career counseling as it is imperative that all three variables be addressed.

John Holland

John Holland stresses the importance of congruence between an individual's personality and his or her relation to the environment (Zunker, 1990). Specifically, Holland addresses the individual's level of satisfaction, acceptance, and success within the work environment. According to Rayman and Atanasoff (1999), an effective theory presents the hypothesis of an issue or event, uses a scientific method of inquiry, and predicts future happenings or occurrences. The key concept entrenched in Holland's theory of career development is that individuals are drawn to a particular vocation by their personality and quest for satisfaction (Zunker, 1990). In this portion of the chapter, we address the effectiveness of Holland's theory of career counseling pertaining to the influence of culture and family structure.

Holland's theory was first presented in the 1950s and has been revisited and revised throughout the years, most recently in 1997 (Chartrand & Walsh, 1999). The theory is predicated on four assumptions (Chartrand & Walsh, 1999; Zunker, 1990):

1. Generally, an individual can identify with one or more of six idealized occupation–interest personality types.
2. There are six corresponding occupational environments.
3. People search for activities and interactions that reflect their personal identities, values, goals, attitudes, and abilities.
4. An individual's behavior is determined by the congruence of the characteristics found in the personality and environment.

Holland's career theory provides a theoretical context in which individuals are assigned to a specific career type on the basis of their corresponding personality style. The theory suggests that individuals who find themselves in an environment incongruent with their personality type will be battling with career indecision (Zunker, 1990). Holland proposes six personality types that reflect his assumptions and work environments that parallel the personality type classifications: Realistic, Investigative, Artistic, Social, Enterprising, and Conventional. The personality and career types are illustrated using a hexagonal model found in Holland's (1992) book *Making Vocational Choices*. The model reflects the relationship between the individual and the environment determining congruence. Holland classifies individuals and their environments, suggesting that they are familiar and compatible to others in that environment (Chartrand & Walsh, 1999).

The quest for self-knowledge is an essential component of Holland's theory (Zunker, 1990). The relationship between self-knowledge and knowledge about a variety of careers is necessary in career decision making. The role of the person–environment influence is to create an understanding of self and the diverse occupational environments that are similar. Holland has been instrumental in the development of criterion or personality inventories related to career counseling. Thus, his theory became a baseline for many of the interventions and the classification system that assists individuals today. Since 1975, Holland has developed instruments and inventories that pair personality types and career possibilities (Holland, Daiger, & Power, 1980; Holland & Gottfredson, 1994). The Self-Directed Search (SDS) was developed to identify personality traits and compare the identified characteristics to career interests in an effort to suggest congruent person–environment options (Zunker, 1990). The SDS is a powerful and effective tool that allows the client to be involved in the career counseling process by facilitating information and understanding (Rayman & Atanasoff, 1999). Within the survey itself, documentation regarding gender, age, ethnic, and racial influences is mentioned as having an impact on the results. Although the SDS has been translated into 20 languages (Holland & Gottfredson, 1994), research is limited in its application with ethnic minorities. From the limited literature available, however, predictive validity has been found for many ethnic minority populations (Bingham & Walsh, 1978; Gade, Fuqua, & Hurlburt, 1984; Kahn & Alvi, 1991; Tay, Hill, & Ward, 1997).

Holland's theory is the basis for at least two other widely used measures of vocational interest: the Strong Interest Inventory and the Campbell Interest and Skill Survey. Fouad, Harmon, and Borgen (1997) surveyed 38,000 racially and ethnically diverse adults and used multidimensional scaling to evaluate data. Results were supported using the Strong Interest Inventory to assess interests of multicultural populations. Although Campbell (1992) stated that he excluded items that were considered insensitive to any demographic category such as race, gender, social class, and ethnic, physical, or geographic groups, there is little research available testing this assertion.

Multicultural Issues and Holland's Theory. Holland's theory has been criticized for not adequately considering the impact of race, social class, and gender influence in career development (Betz & Fitzgerald, 1987; Carter & Swanson, 1990; Fouad, 1993; Fouad, Harmon,

& Hansen, 1994; Fouad & Spreda, 1995; Gottfredson, 1986; Hackett & Watkins, 1995; Ward & Bingham, 1993). Holland addressed diversity issues in his most recent writings on his theory. He stated that the six types of personality that he describes are "a product of a characteristic interaction among a variety of cultural and personal forces including peers, biological heredity, parents, social class, culture, and the physical environment" (Holland, 1997, p. 2).

Ryan, Tracey, and Rounds (1996) evaluated the relations of gender and socioeconomic status (SES) to Holland's six-personality structure (Realistic, Investigative, Artistic, Social, Enterprising, and Conventional) with an African American sample. Contrary to their expectations, it was found that the low-SES African American students fit the model better that the high-SES African American students or a White American sample. Furthermore, Day and Rounds (1998) found when reviewing the research on the applicability of vocational interests across cultures that two observations were documented. The first observation suggests that there is a positive connection between Holland's theory and individuals of diverse cultures with regard to vocational selection (Day & Rounds, 1998; McCrae & Costa, 1997; S. Sue, Keefe, Enomoto, Durvasula, & Chao, 1996). The second observation finds negative results when studies incorporate a possible design flaw: small sample sizes, underrepresentative sampling, controversial responding techniques, or test bias (Baruth & Manning, 1991; Fouad, 1993; Ibrahim, 1985; D. W. Sue & Sue, 1990; Westermeyer, 1987).

The above authors maintained that a large-scale study of the United States multicultural samples now supports the use of Holland's six types model, which is the foundation used in many interest inventories. Men and women in the United States describing themselves as Caucasian, Native American, Asian American, Mexican American, and African American responded to activities in the same pattern, experiencing likes and dislikes for pursuits grouped by Holland's types (Day & Rounds, 1998).

Family Issues and Holland's Theory. The influence of cultural issues has been debated for many years, whereas the family treatment has not been of considerable focus. In addressing the use of Holland's theory of career development across cultures and considering family contexts, the results show conflicting outcomes. It is feasible to see, through the most recent study review by Day and Rounds (1998), that there is an opportunity to utilize the personality inventories across races, genders, socioeconomic backgrounds, and religious affiliations, but the opportunity to include family influences must be accomplished through personal counseling. Essentially, limited resources exist for using Holland's theory with families.

Implications for the Model. Counselors must consider the biases buried in their theoretical orientation as they interpret assessment data, counsel individuals, and offer suggestions and directions for the future. With regard to Holland's theory for implications to the out-of-the-box model, the issues lie in the fact that certain considerations are not evident. Although the influences of the home environment and family systems affect the knowledge and stereotypes found in career choice, Holland's theory focuses on personality without recognizing the impact of family systems. It will be a more difficult fit for the out-of-the-box model; nevertheless, for the future, counselors are urged to apply this theory to their work with clients by considering each client more holistically.

John Krumboltz

The premise that growth takes place as a result of learning and imitating behavior of others is the basis of *social learning theory*. John Krumboltz created a theory of career decision making and development predicated on the social learning/environmental conditions and events, genetic influences, and learning experiences (Krumboltz, 1979). This theory represents one of the earlier applications of Bandura's (1973) social learning theory to career development (Hackett & Lent, 1992), which posits that people acquire their preferences for various activities through a variety of learning experiences. They make sense of these activities because of ideas they have been taught or have learned through experience. Through direct and indirect educational experiences, individuals develop beliefs about themselves and the nature of their world. They then take action on the basis of their beliefs by using skills that they have developed over time (Borow, 1982).

Krumboltz (1979) created 18 propositions with testable hypotheses to include negative and positive influences that could be used to develop research opportunities that support or challenge his theory. These hypotheses are grouped into three major areas: factors influencing career preferences, career decision-making skills, and entry behaviors into educational or occupational alternatives. Factors influencing career preferences are based on vicarious learning, personal experience, and modeling. Career decision-making skills are acquired through positive reinforcement, self-observation, and assessable resources. Lastly, expressed preferences, availability of training opportunities, and cognitive and performance skills are factors that influence a person's behavior toward educational or occupational choice. Interactions among the above factors play a vital role in the career decision-making process.

Mitchell et al. (1999) expanded the theory to include chance or unplanned events as integral components in the career decision-making process. However, career transitions and adaptations are becoming increasingly complex in today's rapidly changing work environment

(Krumboltz, 1998); consequently, people are more susceptible to career disruption. Mitchell et al. (1999) developed the *planned happenstance theory* to include creating and transforming unplanned events into opportunities for learning.

Career counselors can play a crucial role in helping clients create positive chance events on the basis of two concepts: (a) exploration generates chance opportunities for increasing the quality of life, and (b) skills enable people to seize opportunities (Mitchell et al., 1999). According to Mitchell et al., to help clients to seize these opportunities, the career counselor should assist clients in the development of curiosity, persistence, flexibility, optimism, and risk taking. People who adopt the planned happenstance model must be willing to change plans, take risks, work hard to overcome obstacles, and be actively engaged in pursuing their interests.

Multicultural Issues and Krumboltz's Theory. Research suggests that Krumboltz's learning theory of career choice can be expanded across cultures. Hackett and Byars (1996) purported that race and ethnicity influence career efficacy beliefs, interests, and other variables that ultimately predict career choice. For students of color, who may have been actively discouraged from entering career fields such as engineering, self-efficacy expectations may be weakened (Hackett, Casas, Betz, & Rocha-Singh, 1992; Krumboltz, 1979). For example, an African American girl who is performing up to par with her peers in high school courses but receives performance feedback from her teachers that is different from that given to her classmates may experience decreased academic self-efficacy and lowered educational aspirations (Brown & Lent, 1996).

On the basis of their appraisal of the structural inequality and institutionalized discrimination in the United States, African American women may make choices inconsistent with efficacy appraisals because of perceived negative outcomes. Gloria and Hird's (1999) study suggests that ethnic variables are stronger predictors of career decision-making self-efficacy for racial and ethnic minorities than for Whites. Moreover, they indicated that because professional occupations are predominantly occupied and dominated by Whites, racial and ethnic minorities do not believe or expect that their decision making will result in placement in their chosen occupation.

Family Issues and Krumboltz's Theory. Inherent in Krumboltz's social learning theory of career decision making is the importance of family. Family members invariably play a major role in influencing one's career choice. According to Bandura (1973), because parents are usually the most proximal and familiar adult models, they are likely to be one of the most influential sources of information about the world. Several of Krumboltz's (1979) propositions that influence career preference involve observation of valued models. Whether the choice is positively or negatively influenced by family members, children as well as adults value the opinions of those who mean the most to them. Furthermore, just as parents serve as role models for children in the family, so do siblings. Thus, preconceived notions are developed regarding careers and educational preferences based on family members who are considered valued models.

Implications for the Model. Krumboltz's theory of social learning and career decision making introduces several variables, and the process of validation is extremely complex. Concern about the limited applicability of career development theories has grown (Chartrand & Rose, 1996). However, the relationship of ethnic identity and racial salience to career-related efficacy issues is not well known. Underlying environmental, economic, social, and cultural events and conditions impinge upon an individual's learning experiences (Krumboltz, 1979); therefore, implications of the application for the out-of-the-box model is promising. The challenge for counselors will be to provide experiences to clients that will circumvent negative influences in their environment (e.g., role models engaging in criminal activity). As we propel to the 21st century, counselors must be able to identify cultural and familial influences, specifically as it relates to a client's career choice and vocational adaptation. Moreover, counselors must be in tune with their awareness of clients' cultural familial mandates that might contradict social learning theory. In conclusion, because of the emphasis placed on learning experiences in this theory, parents, educators, television executives, and members of the public should pay close attention to the kinds of experiences they provide for young people.

Theory of Work Adjustment

The *theory of work adjustment*, or TWA (Dawis & Lofquist, 1984), seeks to help individuals and work environments establish and maintain a congruous relationship with one another (Bowman, 1998; Dawis, 1996; Dawis & Lofquist, 1984). In TWA terms, this relationship is considered to be one of *correspondence* (Dawis & Lofquist, 1984). Correspondence occurs when the individual's skills and abilities match the needs of the work environment and the work environment's compensatory incentives (e.g., salary, achievement, and security) match the requirements of the individual (Lawson, 1993). Although correspondence is one of the central concepts founded in the theory, what follows is a brief overview of the larger theoretical framework of TWA.

As stated previously, the central principle of the TWA relates to the concept of correspondence; however, understanding how an individual achieves correspondence deserves consideration. Dawis and Lofquist (1984) purported several propositions, which ultimately lead an individual to attain a degree of correspondence within the work environment (Dawis & Lofquist, 1984; Sharf, 1997). Interwoven within the various propositions, other psychological concepts such as skills and abilities, needs and values, and satisfaction are addressed. These particular concepts are viewed as essential if the worker and work environment are to attain mutual correspondence (Bowman, 1998; Breeden, 1993; Dawis & Lofquist, 1984).

In TWA, skills are characterized as abilities, whereas needs are expressed in terms of requirements (Dawis & Lofquist, 1984). Values are those elements that undergird the various need dimensions (Dawis, 1996; Rounds, Henly, Dawis, Lofquist, & Weiss, 1981; Sharf, 1997). Essentially, TWA is based on a reciprocal relationship of the following concepts: (a) abilities of the worker and ability requirements by the work environment, (b) values of the worker and value reinforcers of the work environment, and finally, (c) satisfaction experienced by the worker and satisfactoriness by the work environment (Bowman, 1998; Breeden, 1993; Dawis & Lofquist, 1984; Lofquist & Dawis, 1991). The last concept, satisfaction, is regarded as a central tenet of the TWA that determines the length of time an individual is likely to remain in a particular job (Dawis, 1996). When the worker's abilities and need requirements are commensurate with the work environment's ability requirements and reinforcers, both the worker and the environment are satisfied. Ultimately, the worker and the work environment attain a degree of correspondence, which in turn leads to satisfaction (Bizot & Goldman, 1993; Dawis, 1996; Dawis & Lofquist, 1984; Lawson, 1993).

Each of the theories has both strengths and limitations related to its comprehensiveness. One of the two areas of most interest is how each theory addresses the varied career needs to the diverse population of the United States. What follows is a review of the theories relating to multicultural issues.

Multicultural Issues and TWA. The TWA assumes an individual-differences approach when studying adjustment to the work environment (Dawis & Lofquist, 1984). In other words, TWA is predicated on the concept of differential psychology (i.e., the psychology of individual differences), which may be described as the study of "all the ways individuals differ ... and includes not only a focus on the individual as unique, but also an examination of potential moderators of individual differences such as sex, age, social class, culture, race and special talents" (Tinsley, 1995, p. 342).

The approach taken by TWA is rather comprehensive; however, the moderators to which Tinsley is referring are considered secondary as opposed to primary influences to work adjustment (Dawis, 1996; Sharf, 1997). This is evidenced by Dawis's statement that "TWA as theory focuses on the individual, and gender and minority group status are not defining variables in the theory" (p. 95). Bowman (1998) echoed this sentiment in her article in which she examined career issues faced by minority women. Bowman stated, "to understand why an individual selects a particular career at a specific time it is important to examine the individual's selection process, not the cultural group" (p. 421). This is not to infer that one's culture is not a significant moderator in the selection process. Instead, it is simply stated as a point of reference to indicate that individuals' processes are different; these differences are related more to their individual uniqueness than their standing in a particular group (Dawis & Lofquist, 1984). For example, an Asian American woman may choose a certain career path for different reasons than an African American woman. Although both are considered minority women, according to differential psychology, a more distinct feature lies in their individual differences rather than their collective standing in a group (i.e., both are ethnic minorities and women; Dawis & Lofquist, 1984).

Family Issues and TWA. Since its inception, TWA has evolved into what is now known as *person–environment correspondence* (P-E-C) counseling (Dawis, 1996; Lofquist & Dawis, 1991). This evolution was intended to encompass issues outside the parameters of work (e.g., marriage counseling, family counseling, and addictions counseling; see Lofquist & Dawis, 1991). Essentially, the same tenets found in TWA are also found in P-E-C counseling (e.g., requirements, reinforcers, and satisfaction). Lofquist and Dawis have successfully expanded their theory to include other environments; however, one shortcoming is the theory fails to recognize the interconnectedness of career, multicultural issues, and family systems. Although Dawis and Lofquist (1984) briefly mentioned that correspondence in one environment can affect correspondence in other environments (e.g., family, culture, and leisure), they failed to mention what these effects are or how these effects have an impact on the other environments.

Despite the limited research regarding how these factors are interrelated, one study by Sinacor-Guinn, Akcali, and Fedderus (1999) suggests that there is a correlation between family relationships and job satisfaction among women: that is, the more positive a woman's family environment, the greater likelihood of job satisfaction. Likewise, the more satisfied a woman is in her work environment, the more positive her family environment. Although Sinacor-Guinn et al.'s study indicates the effects family environment has on the work adjustment among women, the literature remains scarce regarding the overall amalgamation of culture, family, and career. In order for TWA to remain viable, there needs to be further research concerning the interrelatedness of these three constructs.

Implications for the Model. As a theory, TWA and P-E-C counseling appear to be quite malleable and seem suitable for adaptation to the out-of-the-box model. In other words, one could conceivably incorporate the effects of family and culture into this theory to better grasp how these two dynamics affect overall correspondence in the work environment. It makes sense that "discorrespondence" in one area of a person's life would affect another area of his or her life. Inasmuch as TWA is flexible, given the fact that the theory is based on differential psychology, it may fail to consider that the preeminence of the individual is a Westernized concept; other cultures are more inclined to place culture and family values before an individual's wants and needs. It is important that counselors be aware of the possibility of this kind of cultural impact and the implications for career selection and satisfaction.

Career Development and Testing

Most theories are validated by research on the populations that they are designed to describe, and this research necessitates the development of instruments to measure concepts. Testing, over the years, has become synonymous with career counseling. In addition to their assistance in validating theories, these test instruments are widely used by counselors to assist clients in their decision making. However, many instruments have come under scrutiny because of the diverse research findings regarding their use with ethnically diverse populations.

Three recent cultural studies—on Black Americans (Swanson, 1992), Hispanic Americans (Fouad & Dancer, 1992), and Asian Americans (Haverkamp, Collins, & Hansen, 1994)—cloud the issues further. Researchers have identified aspects of Holland's hexagonal model that do not accurately reflect the interest structures of ethnic minority groups. Hansen (1992) suggested that the deviations are evidence of important aspects related to minority interests. The study of intragroup variability should be the priority of multicultural research (Padilla, 1994). The tremendous diversity within each of the major ethnic groups in the United States and the use of a cross-racial comparison design may mask important within-group differences.

Seligman (1994) proposed that the solution to dealing with cultural bias does not mean eliminating all tests or even concentrating on developing inventories that are culture free. Rather, her solution involves "refining established tests and developing new ones that have demonstrated their validity regardless of the background or gender of the test takers and that does not perpetuate discriminatory attitudes and limitations" (p. 91). In addition, as Watkins and Campbell (1990) stated, "Future efforts in these areas will focus on (a) using and interpreting available tests within the context of cultural boundaries, and (b) developing and validating culturally specific tests and assessment methods" (p. 193).

Hansen (1992) challenged researchers to continue to explore and develop interest inventories that accurately reflect diverse cultural groups. It is clear that, as a multicultural society, we need to develop assessment instruments that are valid and reliable for a diverse, cross-cultural population. "Counselors today have a body of knowledge that underlines the impact of race, gender, and class…and with this knowledge, counselors have the potential to redress some of the inequities perpetuated by our economic and educational systems" (Hawks & Muha, 1991, p. 253). Counselors need to remember to not overemphasize assessments and to consider the results in connection with other information. Harmon, Hansen, Borgen, and Hammer (1994) emphasized, "culture must be incorporated as a variable when interpreting the inventory to clients" (p. 275).

Major publishers are alert to the importance of issues of diversity and generally take steps to maximize the effectiveness of an instrument for a variety of groups. There must be a sensitivity for legitimate concerns of people from different demographic classifications: racial, ethnic, religious, sexual preference, and handicapping conditions. Nonetheless, it is safe to say that no publisher can possibly gather evidence on the appropriateness of an instrument for all possible groups, and some publishers do not gather sufficient data for any groups. Federal legislation, such as the 1974 Family Educational Rights and Privacy Act (The Buckley Amendment); the Education of All Handicapped Children Act of 1975; the 1978 Guidelines for Assessment of Sex Bias and Sex Fairness in Career Interest Inventories; the 1979 Vocational Education Programs Guidelines for Eliminating Discrimination and Denial of Services on the Basis of Race, Color, National Origin, Sex, and Handicap; and the Individuals with Disability Act of 1990 govern and influence the use of tests. These and other laws were designed to protect oppressed and underrepresented groups and prohibit the use of tests in ways that would limit a person's opportunities in educational or vocational programs (Gelberg & Chojinacki, 1996; Kapes & Whitfield, 2001).

Professional associations also provide direction for the appropriate use of assessment instruments in career counseling. In 1999, the American Psychological Association (APA) published the Standards for Educational Psychological Testing. These standards were developed in conjunction with the American Educational Research Association and the National Council for Measurement in Education. APA has also published Rights and Responsibilities of Test Takers: Guidelines and Responsibilities. The American Counseling Association published its policy statement in the document Responsibilities of Users of Standardized Tests (Kapes & Whitfield, 2001). There remain, however, groups that do not receive any national protection, such as gays, lesbian, and bisexuals.

Resources that explore the career needs of specific groups, such as Gelberg and Chojinacki's (1996) Career and Life Planning With Gay, Lesbian, and Bisexual Persons, can provide a wealth of information to assist the counselor in making better assessment choices. For example, Gelberg and Chojinacki provided a chapter reviewing the major career theories from the gay, lesbian, and bisexual perspective and how assessments can be adapted to meet the needs of these clients.

Overall, it is the responsibility of those selecting instruments to determine whether data exist pertaining to the appropriateness of the instrument for a particular group. Professional use of assessment instruments requires a multicultural sensitivity to legal, social, cultural, and ethical factors.

§◦ Theories of Family Therapy ◦§

Despite the fact that almost all clients have families, a family approach to counseling has gained popularity very slowly. Counselors and psychologists tend to conceptualize and treat emotional problems as problems of the individual. The emergence of family therapy brought an awareness of the reciprocal nature of problems—that clients'"problems" affect their families as much as their families can affect the problem. Those in the profession became more open to viewing the client as a part of a system and recognizing that the system is only as healthy and as strong as its weakest member (Gladding, 1998).

Multicultural and Career Issues in Family Theories

Not much focus has been placed on culture in the family literature. Bean and Crane (1996) reviewed publications of the leading family journals over a 10-year period (1983–1993) and found that only 9.4% of the articles focused on racial and ethnic minorities or specific minority issues. Most of those publications were designed to describe ethnic minority families or to give suggestions on treating them. Most of this work is addressed in other chapters of this book. Almost no research has been done on the applicability of family therapy to ethnic minority clients. Similarly, although the career theories give some attention to family issues (even if it is limited), the treatment of career issues in theories of family therapy is almost nonexistent.

In this section, we discuss the ways in which various theories of family therapy address culture and career issues. The theories include structural family therapy, strategic family therapy, narrative family therapy, and solution-focused family therapy. We have selected these theories because of their prominence among practicing counselors and because they can most feasibly adapt to our family, culture, and career model.

However, other family theories are covered in the case studies of this book. After a brief review of the selected theories, we look at the treatment of culture and career issues in these theories. Because of the limited amount of literature available on the treatment of these issues in family theories, we collapse them into two categories: modernists and postmodernists.

Structural Family Therapy. As with most models of family systems therapy, Salvador Minuchin's structural family therapy purports that "human problems can only be understood and treated in context" (Colapinto, 2000) and that context is usually the family. Minuchin believes families relate to one another in an organized manner and that this organization creates the structure within which its members must conform (Sharf, 2000). Families typically come to counseling when the family structure runs into difficulty. Structural family therapists believe that the family is comprised of several distinct subsystems: spousal (husband and wife), parental (father and mother), child (siblings), and extended family (grandparents, aunts, uncles, close relatives, or friends; Corey, 2001). Problems occur when members cross boundaries and intrude on one another's subsystems (e.g., parents get involved in their children's subsystem by dictating what they should play and who should go first). Boundaries help the members of each subsystem maintain its identity; when boundaries are broken, family members tend to become overly involved in each other's lives. Minuchin calls this over-involvement *enmeshment* (Sharf, 2000).

Structural family therapists help families with structural difficulties to develop appropriate boundaries by changing the stereotyped patterns of interaction and creating a new structure. Change is usually brought about by an active therapist joining the family and making direct interventions to interrupt old ways of interacting and eliminating the family's ineffective structure.

Strategic Family Therapy. Strategic family therapy has been most influence by the contributions of Jay Haley, who himself was influenced by Minuchin and Milton Erickson (Sharf, 2000). Haley focuses less on the structure of the family and more on the family's patterns of relating to one another to solve problems. He believes that families become dysfunctional when those relational patterns no longer solve family problems but exist only to protect the family from disintegration. It is the therapist's job to promote change by giving the family directives that will interrupt dysfunctional relational patterns. Once disrupted, the family members can find new ways of relating that will help them once again solve problems. The therapy is focused on problem solution: The problem is viewed as real and is solved (Keim, 2000). Although the process of therapy is different in each family, the therapist always attends to issues of behavioral sequences in the family, hierarchy (who has the power), and metaphor. The counselor focuses on who is doing what to whom under what conditions. The therapist acts as the expert, is in charge of the sessions, and designs intervention strategies that are appropriate for that particular family.

Narrative Family Therapy. Michael White (an Australian) has emerged as a major contributor to narrative family therapy in the United States. Narrative therapy's philosophy of social constructivism emphasizes "the ways in which people make meaning in social relations" (Corey, 2001, p. 428). Every individual has a unique perspective of every situation he or she encounters. An individual's interpretation of life events (his or her story) creates meaning in that person's life. Individuals also live in a family system that itself has a communal story (narrative) that outlines the family's values and meanings. The family's communal narratives are embedded in dominant narratives of the larger systems of culture and society. Because the dominant culture's narratives are designed to perpetuate its own values and meanings, White (1992, cited in Corey, 2001) believes that individuals and families can be oppressed by these stories. The goal of narrative family therapy is to help families "re-establish their freedom from the oppression of external problems and the dominant stories of larger systems" (Corey, 2001, p. 431).

By treating the client family's stories as truth and believing the client is the expert, narrative therapists use conversational questioning and a "not knowing" stance to assist clients in expressing what is not said (Anderson & Goolishian, 1992). Therapists use externalizing questions to separate the problem from the individuals. The problem, not the individual family member, becomes the enemy. Problems may be labeled "anger" or "anxiety," and family members are encouraged to talk about anger and how it affects them. By making the problem a separate entity external to the family, members can discuss it and work on it, and the therapist can help the clients to create alternative stories (reauthoring) that emphasize the strengths, special abilities, and aspirations of the family (Sharf, 2000).

Solution-Focused Family Therapy. The major contributors to solution-focused family therapy are Steve deShazer and Bill O'Hanlon, who were also influenced by Milton Erickson. Although their approaches differ, the basic premise of the theory is in its name, which focuses on solving the client's problems. Clients are not asked to discover why there is a problem, nor are they to figure out how the problem arose. The lock-and-key metaphor is used for client problems—the problem is the lock and counselors must help clients find the key, or the solution (Gladding, 1998). Counselors do not focus on the details of the family's history because causal understanding is not necessary. They believe the clients want to change, and it is the counselor's duty to find out how to make that happen. Finally, the counselor believes that only a small change is

like RET

necessary for change to occur in order for clients' families to be reinforced and to start approaching their lives differently. According to
Gladding, clients are encouraged to be creative and to generate novel
approaches that might be applicable to a number of situations. The novel
approaches are called *skeleton keys* (Gladding, 1998). Clients are viewed
by the counselor as cooperative, and the counselor challenges them and
sets up expectations for change. The techniques used by counselors
include (a) messages sent by the counselor to the client giving compli-
ments, suggestions, or clues; (b) descriptive questions that ask what happened before counseling; (c) miracle questions that ask what will happen
if the problem disappeared overnight; and (d) exception questions that
ask when is this not a problem, coping questions, and scaling (sizing up
the level of change; Corey, 2001; Sharf, 2000). Treatment ends when the
client's goals have been reached.

Family Approaches to Cultural and Career Issues

Whereas strategic and structural family therapies subscribe to the modernist notion that there is one universal truth that can be discovered and
explained, the narrative approaches and solution-focused therapy represent the postmodern perspective of subjective reality: Truth is whatever a given individual perceives to be true (Corey, 2001). Therefore,
instead of a single universal reality of the modernists, postmodernist
thinking allows for multiple realities. There is a more thorough discussion of postmodern philosophy later in this book.

Modernist Family Approaches. The modernist theories (structural and strategic family counseling) are considered by many to be
heavily value-oriented with values that do not necessarily apply across
cultures and need to be modified to be appropriate for ethnically different clients and women, in general. For example, structural family therapy has been criticized for its patriarchal view of the family, its
imposition of the point of view that the man is in charge of the family,
and blaming the mother for the child's problems. Also, Minuchin has
been criticized for his stance on boundaries and enmeshment because
there are many cultures in which the subsystems overlap intentionally
and interdependence, not enmeshment, is encouraged (Goldenberg &
Goldenberg, 2000). Whereas some cultures may believe in the expert-
ness of the strategic family therapists, others may resent the intrusion of
someone outside the family giving instructions to family members.

Extrapolating from what we know about theses theories, structural
and strategic family therapies could be adapted to include career issues.
For example, the family may have so much disruption that a member of
the family finds it hard to do well in his or her job. Therefore, changing
family dynamics to the point that there is more harmony in the family

will assist with the person's career. On the other hand, a family member's problems with his or her career may upset that person's behavior in the family to such an extent that changes will have to be made not only in the family but also in the individual family member's occupation. In these scenarios, it would be appropriate for structural and strategic family therapists to engage in career counseling with the family.

Postmodern Family Approaches. Postmodern approaches (narrative and solution-focused therapy) promote multiple realities and multiple perspectives. Although this seems to be a step in the right direction, in the real world, there is still racism, sexism, classism, and many other "isms" that have an effect on clients (Peterson & Gonzalez, 2000). These are not co-constructed realities. Their perceptions are real and not only to the clients. Postmodernists need to address the "realness" of the problems with their clients. In addition, the language of some of the postmodernists can seem coded and politically laden, which can get in the way of the working relationship between client and counselor.

The postmodern approaches tend to more closely address multiple perspectives within families than the modernist approaches and therefore could more easily involve career issues. With solution-focused therapy, there may be a tendency to settle too soon on the problem. To be effective, counselors must explore all the possibilities to discover if career is the real issue with clients before setting goals. This careful exploration will help clients to see a broader picture of their problems and make informed choices about what they want to change.

Future of Family Therapies

Many of the family therapies can be adapted to be more inclusive to ethnic groups. The culturally sensitive and competent counselor will be able to make those adjustments needed to be effective and helpful to his or her client. The greater challenge will be for the theories to be more inclusive of career development. Every day, families face issues that are directly related to the work life of family members. In the 21st century, counselors must develop competence in career counseling and must make a genuine effort to ask for and address these issues in session.

꿈 Summary 꿈

In this chapter, we briefly overviewed a small group of popular and well-known theories of career and family counseling. We would be remiss if we did not mention one of the newest theories of career counseling that might be especially relevant to the out-of-the-box model: social cognitive career theory (SCCT). Bandura's (1977, 1986, 1997) work on social cognitive theory is the foundation for SCCT. Lent, Brown, and Hackett (1994) applied Bandura's thinking to career counseling. SCCT examines the relationships and interactions between what is called cognitive person variable (e.g., self-efficacy and goals) and contextual variables or other aspects of the person and his or her environment (e.g., gender, ethnicity, and barriers). This concept gives equal value to factors both outside and within the person. Individuals may have strong cognitive person variables that influence their career choices and development, but they also have extraperson or contextual variables that may enhance or restrict their personal agency (Lent, Brown, & Hackett, 2000). SCCT appears to encourage counselors to think about their career clients in multiple perspectives—individual attributes, contextual influences, and the interaction between these variables—and is very adaptable to the out-of-the-box model. Readers are encouraged to learn more about SCCT by reading the complete description of the SCCT model (Lent et al., 1994).

We have barely scratched the surfaces of the theories we have reviewed and are aware that, by briefly summarizing them, we have not done them the justice they deserve. It was our intention to make the reader aware of the strengths and weaknesses of these theories when applying the out-of-the-box model. We are certain that practitioners in the field who use these theories have found ways to adapt them to their clientele and their own personal style. We hope we have alerted them to further adaptations that will be needed as the diversity of their clientele and the complexity of client problems increase.

ॐ References ॐ

Anderson, H., & Goolishian, H. (1992). The client is the expert: A not-knowing approach to therapy. In S. McNamee & K. J. Gergen (Eds.), *Therapy as social construction* (pp. 25–39). Newbury Park, CA: Sage.

Bandura, A. (1973). *Social learning theory*. Englewood Cliffs, NJ: Prentice Hall.

Bandura, A. (1977). Self-efficacy: Toward a unifying theory of behavioral change. *Psychological Review, 87*, 191–215.

Bandura, A. (1986). *Social foundations of thought and action*. Englewood Cliffs, NJ: Prentice Hall.

Bandura, A. (1997). *Self efficacy: The exercise of control*. New York: Freeman.

Baruth, L. G., & Manning, M. L. (1991). *Multicultural counseling and psychotherapy: A lifespan perspective*. New York: Merrill.

Bean, R., & Crane, D. R. (1996). Marriage and family therapy research with ethnic minorities: Current status. *American Journal of Family Therapy, 24*, 3–8.

Betz, E. (1984). A study of career patterns of women college graduates. *Journal of Vocational Behavior, 24*, 249–263.

Betz, N. E., & Fitzgerald, L. F. (1987). *The career psychology of women*. Orlando, FL: Academic Press.

Betz, N. E., & Fitzgerald, L. F. (1995). Career assessment and intervention with racial and ethnic minorities. In F.T. L. Leong (Ed.), *Career development and vocational behavior of racial and ethnic minorities* (pp. 263–279). Hillsdale, NJ: Erlbaum.

Bingham, R. F., & Walsh, W. B. (1978). Concurrent validity of Holland's theory for college-degreed Black working women. *Journal of Vocational Behavior, 13,* 242–250.

Bizot, E. B., & Goldman, S. H. (1993). Prediction of satisfactoriness and satisfaction: An 8-year follow up. *Journal of Vocational Behavior, 43,* 19–29.

Borow, H. (1982). Career development theory and instrumental outcomes of career guidance: a critique. In J. D. Krumboltz & D. A. Hamel (Eds.), *Assessing career development* (pp. 18–40). Mountain View, CA: Mayfield.

Bowman, S. L. (1998). Minority women and career adjustment. *Journal of Career Assessment, 6,* 417–431.

Breeden, S. A. (1993). Job and occupational change as a function of occupational correspondence and job satisfaction. *Journal of Vocational Behavior, 43,* 30–45.

Brown, S. D., & Lent, R. W. (1996). A social cognitive framework for career choice counseling. *Career Development Quarterly, 44,* 354–365.

Campbell, D. P. (1992). *Campbell Interest and Skill Survey.* Minneapolis, MN: National Computer Systems.

Carter, R. T., & Swanson, J. L. (1990). *Minorities in higher education: Tenth annual status report.* Washington, DC: American Council on Education.

Chartrand, J. M., & Rose, M. L. (1996). Career interventions for at-risk populations: incorporating social cognitive influences. *Career Development Quarterly, 44,* 341–353.

Chartrand, J., & Walsh, B. W. (1999). What should we expect from congruence? *Journal of Vocational Behavior, 55,* 136–146.

Colapinto, J. (2000). Structural family therapy. In A. Hone (Ed.), *Family counseling and therapy* (pp. 140–169). Itasca, IL: Peacock.

Corey, G. (2001). *Theory and practice of counseling and psychotherapy.* Belmont: CA: Brooks-Cole/Wadsworth.

Dawis, R. V. (1996). The theory of work adjustment and person-environment-correspondence counseling. In D. Brown, L. Brooks, & Associates (Eds.), *Career choice and development* (3rd ed., pp. 75–120). San Francisco: Jossey-Bass.

Dawis, R.V., & Lofquist, L. H. (1984). *A psychological theory of work adjustment: An individual differences model and its application.* Minneapolis: University of Minnesota Press.

Day, S. X., & Rounds, J. (1998). Universality of vocational interest structure among racial and ethnic minorities. *American Psychologist, 53,* 728–736.

Fouad, N. A. (1993). Cross-cultural vocational assessment. *Career Development Quarterly, 42,* 4–13.

Fouad, N. A. (1994). Annual review 1991–1993: Vocational choice, decision-making, assessment, and intervention. *Journal of Vocational Behavior, 45,* 125–176.

Fouad, N. A., & Dancer, L. S. (1992). Cross-cultural structure of interests: Mexico and the United States. *Journal of Vocational Behavior, 40,* 129–143.

Fouad, N. A., Harmon, L. W., & Borgen, F. H. (1997). Structure of interests of employed male and female members of U.S. racial-ethnic minority and non-minority groups. *Journal of Counseling Psychology, 44,* 339-345.

Fouad, N. A., Harmon, L. W., & Hansen, J. C. (1994). Cross-cultural use of the Strong. In L. W. Harmon, J. C. Hansen, F. H. Borgen, & A. L. Hammer (Eds.), *Strong Interest Inventory: Applications and technical guide* (pp. 255-280). Palo Alto, CA: Consulting Psychologists Press.

Fouad, N. A., & Keeley, T. J. (1992). The relationship between attitudinal and behavioral aspects of career maturity. *Career Development Quarterly, 40,* 257-271.

Fouad, N. A., & Spreda, S. L. (1995). Use of interest inventories with special populations: Women and minority groups. *Journal of Career Assessment, 3,* 453-468.

Gade, E. M., Fuqua, D., & Hurlburt, G. (1984). Use of the self-directed search with Native Americans. *Journal of Counseling Psychology, 31,* 584-587.

Gelberg, S., & Chojinacki, J. T. (1996). *Career and life planning with gay, lesbian, and bisexual persons.* Alexandria, VA: American Counseling Association.

Gladding, S. T. (1998). *Family therapy: History, theory, and practice.* Upper Saddle River, NJ: Prentice Hall.

Gloria, A. M., & Hird, J. S. (1999). Influences of ethnic and non-ethnic variables on the career decision making self-efficacy of college students. *Career Development Quarterly, 48,* 157-174.

Goldenberg, I., & Goldenberg, H. (2000). *Family therapy: An overview* (5th ed.). Belmont, CA: Brooks-Cole/Wadsworth.

Gottfredson, L. S. (1986). Special groups and the beneficial use of vocational interest inventories. In W. B. Walsh & S. H. Osipow (Eds.), *Advances in vocational psychology: Vol. 1. The assessment of interests* (pp. 127-198). Hillsdale, NJ: Erlbaum.

Hackett, G., & Byars, A. M. (1996). Social cognitive theory and career development of African American women. *Career Development Quarterly, 44,* 322-340.

Hackett, G., Casas, J. M., Betz, N. E., & Rocha-Singh, I. A. (1992). Gender, ethnicity, and social cognitive factors predicting the academic achievement of students in engineering. *Journal of Counseling Psychology, 39,* 527-538.

Hackett, G., & Lent, R. W. (1992). Theoretical advances and current inquiry in career psychology. In S. D. Brown & R. W. Lent (Eds.), *Handbook of counseling psychology* (2nd ed., pp. 419-451). New York: Wiley.

Hackett, G., & Watkins, C. E. (1995). Research in career assessment: Abilities, interests, decision making and career development. In W. B. Walsh & S. H. Osipow (Eds.), *Advances in vocational psychology: Theory, research, and practice* (2nd ed., pp. 181-215). Mahwah, NJ: Erlbaum.

Hansen, J. C. (1992). Does enough evidence exist to modify Holland's theory to accommodate the individual differences of diverse populations? *Journal of Vocational Behavior, 40,* 188-103.

Harmon, L. W., Hansen, J. C., Borgen, F. H., & Hammer, A. L. (1994). *Strong Interest Inventory applications and technical guide.* Palo Alto, CA: Consulting Psychologists Press.

Haverkamp, B. E., Collins, R. C., & Hansen, J. C. (1994). Structure of interest of Asian-American college students. *Journal of Counseling Psychology, 41*, 256-264.

Hawks, B. K., & Muha, D. (1991). Facilitating the career development of minorities: Doing it differently this time. *Career Development Quarterly, 39*, 251-260.

Herr, E. L. (1997). Super's life-span, life-space approach and its outlook for refinement. *Career Development Quarterly, 45*, 238-246.

Holland, J. L. (1992). *Making vocational choices: A theory of vocational personalities and work environments* (2nd ed.). Odessa, FL: Psychological Assessment Resources.

Holland, J. L. (1997). *Making vocational choices: A theory of vocational personalities and work environments* (3rd ed.). Odessa, FL: Psychological Assessment Resources.

Holland, J. L., Daiger, D. C., & Power, P. G. (1980). Some diagnostic scales for research in decision-making and personality: Identity, information, and barriers. *Journal of Personality and Social Psychology, 39*, 1191-1200.

Holland, J. L., & Gottfredson, F. D. (1994). *Career attitudes and strategies inventory: An inventory for understanding adult careers*. Odessa, FL: Psychological Assessment Resources.

Ibrahim, F. A. (1985). Effective cross-cultural counseling and psychotherapy: A framework. *The Counseling Psychologist, 12*, 625-638.

Kapes, J. T., & Whitfield, E. A. (Eds.). (2001). *A counselor's guide to career assessment instruments*. Columbus, OH: National Career Development Association.

Keim, J. (2000). Strategic family therapy: The Washington model. In A. Hone (Ed.), *Family counseling and therapy* (pp. 170-207). Itasca, IL: Peacock

Khan, S. B., & Alvi, S. A. (1991). The structure of Holland's typology: A study in non-Western culture. *Journal of Cross-Cultural Psychology, 22*, 283-292.

Krumboltz, J. D. (1979). A social learning theory of career decision-making. In A. M. Mitchell, G. B. Jones, & J. D. Krumboltz (Eds.), *Social learning and career decision making* (pp. 19-49). Cranston, RI: Carroll Press.

Krumboltz, J. D. (1998). Serendipity is not serendipitous. *Journal of Counseling Psychology, 45*, 390-392.

Lawson, L. (1993). Theory of work adjustment personality constructs. *Journal of Vocational Behavior, 43*, 46-57.

Lent, R. W., Brown, S. D., & Hackett, G. (1994). Toward a unifying social cognitive theory of career and academic interest, choice and performance. *Journal of Vocational Behavior, 45*, 79-122.

Lent, R. W., Brown, S. D., & Hackett, G. (2000). Contextual supports and barriers to career choice: A social cognitive analysis. *Journal of Counseling Psychology, 47*, 36-49.

Lofquist, L. H., & Dawis, R. V. (1991). *Essentials of person-environment-correspondence counseling*. Minneapolis: University of Minnesota Press.

Lubinski, D., & Dawis, R. V. (1995). *Assessing individual differences in human behavior*. Palo Alto, CA: Davies-Black.

McCrae, R. R., & Costa, P. T. (1997). Personality trait structure as a human universal. *American Psychologist, 52*, 509-516.

Mitchell, K. E., Levin, A. S., & Krumboltz, J. D. (1999). Planned happenstance: constructing unexpected career opportunities. *Journal of Counseling and Development, 77*, 115-124.

Padilla, A. M. (1994). Ethnic minority scholars, research, and mentoring: Current and future issues. *Educational Researchers, 23*, 24-27.

Peterson, N., & Gonzalez, R. C. (2000). *The role of work in people's lives: Applied career counseling and vocational psychology.* Belmont, CA: Brooks-Cole/Wadsworth.

Rayman, J., & Atanasoff, L. (1999). Holland's theory and career intervention: The power of the hexagon. *Journal of Vocational Behavior, 55*, 114-126.

Rodriquez, M., & Blocher, D. (1988). A comparison of two approaches to enhancing career maturity in Puerto Rican college women. *Journal of Counseling Psychology, 35*, 275-280.

Rounds, J. B., Henly, G. A., Dawis, R. V., Lofquist, L. H., & Weiss, D. J. (1981). *Manual for the Minnesota Importance Questionnaire: A measure for vocational needs.* Minneapolis: University of Minnesota, Department of Psychology.

Ryan, J. M., Tracey, T. J. G., & Rounds, J. (1996). Generalizability of Holland's structure of vocational interests across ethnicity, gender and socioeconomic status. *Journal of Counseling Psychology, 43*, 330-337.

Salomone, P. R. (1996). Tracing Super's theory of vocational development: A 40-year retrospective. *Journal of Career Development, 22*, 167-184.

Seligman, L. (1994). *Developmental career counseling and assessment* (2nd ed.). Thousand Oaks, CA: Sage.

Sharf, R. S. (1997). *Applying career development theory to counseling.* Pacific Grove, CA: Brooks/Cole.

Sharf, R. S. (2000). *Theories of psychotherapy and counseling: Concepts and cases.* Belmont, CA: Brooks-Cole/Wadsworth.

Sinacore-Guinn, A. L., Akcali, F. O., & Fedderus, S. W. (1999). Employed women: Family and work—reciprocity and satisfaction. *Journal of Career Development, 25*, 187-201.

Sue, D. W., & Sue, D. (1990). *Counseling the culturally different: Theory and practice* (2nd ed.). New York: Wiley.

Sue, S., Keefe, D., Enomoto, K., Durvasula, R. S., & Chao, R. (1996). Asian American and White college students' performance on the MMPI-2. In J. N. Butcher (Ed.), *International adaptations of the MMPI-2: Research and clinical applications* (pp. 206-218). Minneapolis: University of Minnesota Press.

Super, D. E. (1957). *The psychology of careers.* New York: Harper & Row.

Super, D. E. (1980). A life-span, life-space approach to career development. *Journal of Vocational Behavior, 16*, 282-298.

Super, D. E. (1985). Career counseling across cultures. In P. Pedersen (Ed.), *Handbook of cross-cultural counseling and therapy* (pp. 11-20). Westport, CT: Greenwood Press.

Super, D. E. (1990). A life-span, life-space approach to career development. In D. Brown & L. Brooks (Eds.), *Career choice and development* (pp. 192-234). San Francisco: Jossey-Bass.

Swanson, J. L. (1992). The structure of vocational interests for African-American college students. *Journal of Vocational Behavior, 40*, 144-157.

Tay, K. K., Hill, J.A., & Ward, C. M. (1997, August). *Factorial and structural validity of Holland's hexagonal model for an Asian student population.* Paper presented at the annual meeting of the American Psychological Association, Chicago.

Tinsley, H. E. A. (1995). The Minnesota counseling psychologist as a broadly trained applied psychologist. In D. Lubinski & R. V. Dawis (Eds.), *Assessing individual differences in human behavior* (pp. 341-356). Palo Alto, CA: Davies-Black.

Ward, C. M., & Bingham, R. P. (1993). Career assessment of ethnic minority women. *Journal of Career Assessment, 1,* 246-257.

Watkins, C. E., & Campbell, V. L. (1990). Testing and assessing in counseling psychology: Contemporary developments and issues. *The Counseling Psychologist, 18,* 189-197.

Westermeyer, J. (1987). Cultural factors in clinical assessment. *Journal of Consulting and Clinical Psychology, 55,* 471-478.

Zunker, V. G. (1990). *Career counseling: Applied concepts of life planning.* Pacific Grove, CA: Brooks/Cole.

Part III

❧

Treatment Strategies

❧ Chapter 4 ❧

Strategies for Counseling Family One: The Vargas family

Nancy Ochs and Kathy M. Evans

Veronica Vargas is referred to the college counseling center by her residence hall director. Over the course of her first year, Veronica has become more withdrawn from hall activities and, according to her roommate, has begun to miss class. Last weekend Veronica's family came to visit, but the visit ended with Veronica and her father screaming at each other. Veronica wants to change her major from nursing to medicine but her father is against it.

After much reluctance, Veronica agrees to attend counseling sessions. Her first words focus on how counseling is not something that "her family does" and that she feels embarrassed and ashamed to be there. She states that her mother is a social worker and that she associates counseling with people who have "real problems."

In the discussion, Veronica discloses that her biggest concern is that she wants to change her major so that she can become a pediatric oncologist. Her father, George, refuses to consider such a career for her, suggesting that nursing is "close enough" to the medical field and that he will not financially support the extra schooling required for medicine. Confidentially, Veronica shares that her mother, Sarah, has been secretly encouraging her to shift to medicine. She says that when at home, she has heard her parents fight about what career is "appropriate" in the Vargas family for "George's oldest daughter." Veronica also states that her boyfriend, a junior at another university, is a pre-med student and that she thinks it would be wonderful if they have a career in common.

Veronica's father's family immigrated to the United States from Guatemala when he was 6 years old. At 49, he is a retired military man. During his service commitment, George completed a degree in accounting, and he is now a certified public accountant and has been employed by the same company for 7 years. George is the oldest of four sons and the only one to graduate from college. His brothers work in the family's restaurant supply business in San Francisco. George was raised in what he describes as a traditional Latino family with strong affiliation to the Catholic church. Since his marriage, he has not attended services and has allowed his connection to the church to deteriorate. This "lapse in faith," as George's parents describe it, is also condemned by George's grandmother, 88, who will speak only to George when the Vargas family visits, and then only in Spanish. She has yet to acknowledge Sarah, except as "that woman."

Veronica's mother, 42, is a social worker in a community mental health center. She was raised in a Jewish home but, according to Veronica, grew away from her faith and has not attended a synagogue service in many years. George and Sarah met in 1980 when George was stationed at Pearl Harbor and Sarah was employed as a base social worker. They dated for about a year and married in a civil ceremony in Hawaii, but only Sarah's mother, Annette, attended the wedding. George's parents (Luis and Maria) live in San Francisco and could not attend the wedding. They have met Sarah only once, when the couple returned to live in Atlanta. Sarah has worked on and off as a social worker, depending on where they were stationed while George was in the military. She is the only child of two professional parents: Annette, a clinical social worker, and Vern, an architect.

Veronica has a younger sister, Annie, who is 15, and a younger brother, Lewis, 12. During high school, Veronica maintained excellent grades, worked in a day-care center, and volunteered at a local hospital on the pediatric wards. She recalls having arguments with her father because he was worried that the demands of the patients would overwhelm her, and he encouraged her instead to spend more time with her boyfriend and girlfriends. He complained, with some pride, Veronica hoped, that she worked too hard and did not have enough fun. She remembers how strange it was to have a father who wanted her to spend more time with boyfriends and friends when all of her friends' parents complained when their daughters did exactly that.

We use the out-of-the-box model in this chapter to address Veronica's concerns. The first step is to understand Veronica's perspective by letting her tell her story.

❧ Understanding the Client's Worldview ❦

The out-of-the-box model specifies that the counselor should assess the client's problem from multiple perspectives, listen for client priorities, and then make an assessment of the client's life focal point. There are a number of perspectives that have an impact on Veronica's emotional state at this time. These perspectives make up her worldview that includes her view of her culture, her family, her career decision and ability status, her gender, and her age.

Culture

It is apparent that Veronica's family has mostly assimilated to the dominant European American culture and has raised her to accept and embrace it with all its characteristics and values. Perhaps because of the family's cultural mix, acculturating to the dominant American culture seemed to be the best compromise for her parents. Typically, the parents in bicultural and biracial families want to live in a way that does not call attention to their differentness (Okun, 1996). Often the military (which has many biracial and bicultural families) provides the type of multicultural environment that allows for easier acceptance. It also appears that neither George nor Sarah imposed his and her own cultural upbringing on Veronica and her siblings, nor did either of them encourage the children to have interest in their cultural heritage. Furthermore, because the Vargas children were not visibly different from other White children, identification with the dominant culture was fairly easy.

Although Veronica's parents made special efforts to suppress the influence of their own cultural upbringing on their children, their cultural heritage is still a part of themselves. There is no doubt that Veronica has heard stories of her parents' childhoods. However, she views these stories not as her heritage but simply as history.

Family

Veronica's perspective is that a family consists of two parents and their biological children. Because her family had to move around a great deal, they learned that they had to depend on one another. The extended family was abstract—people's names on cards, letters, and telephones. From her current point of view, her father is being stubborn, condescending, sexist, and mean. She is equally angry with her mother, who supports her only in secrecy. Although the case example does not give this information, it appears that Veronica has been an obedient, loving child—one who was comfortable living the military lifestyle, who enjoyed a happy relationship with her father, and who rarely questioned her father's authority. She now feels abandoned by her family when she really needs it for one of the most important decisions of her life.

Career and Abilities

In her story, Veronica sees herself as a bright, achieving person with a limitless future. She believes that because of her talents she should be able to do whatever she desires. In fact, this is the message that both her parents have given her since she was a small child. However, now that she has reached adulthood, Veronica discovers that at least one of her parents believes that there are limits to what she should achieve, and she is angry with him for it. Veronica has made a clear career choice but is torn by the conflicting messages she is receiving from her family. She has proved that she has the academic ability, the interest, and, with her father's financial support, the money to pursue a career as a doctor.

A particularly salient point is that Veronica has earlier work experience in a pediatrics ward. Her interest in becoming a pediatric oncologist has a base that she has to some extent already tested.

Gender

Veronica does not see that her gender should have any influence on her career decision. She realizes that she wants to change from a traditionally female occupation to a traditionally male occupation but does not believe that the change should be problematic. Veronica now recognizes that a nontraditional occupation (especially one with long, protracted educational requirements) is a problem for her father. She believes he will support her only if she pursues a traditional female career, gets married, and (in her mind) becomes a demure homemaker with a part-time job to keep her busy. She sees this as the pattern her mother's career has taken for so many years, in so many places.

As far as we can tell from the information given, Veronica believes that her academic abilities are equal to her boyfriend's and, therefore, she is capable of pursuing as demanding a career. Furthermore, she may think that if they pursue a common career, many of the difficulties encountered by her mother might be avoided. It is likely that even though her mother has been Veronica's primary female role model, Veronica has had a great deal of exposure to women in the military, including women doctors. Perhaps she observed that these women were successfully managing multiple roles of doctor, wife, and mother.

Age

Veronica has reached the age when the dominant culture expects her to spread her wings and become independent of her nuclear family. She is hesitant to take off because her family has been her only support, and it appears to her that she will lose that support if she exercises her independence.

☞ Lifestyle Focal Point ☜

It appears that Veronica's focal point is as much career related as it is family related; in this case, the counselor must concentrate on both these areas. Once the counselor gets deeper into the problem, other issues might surface that include culture and gender issues. Veronica has made a career decision but may hesitate to implement it because she needs to find a way to bring her family together on this decision. In the model, the focal point in the middle would be family and career. Now that the counselor has an understanding of Veronica's focal point, the impact of the counselor's own cultural values must be explored.

❧ Impact of Counselor's Values ❧

The key values in Veronica's case involve attitudes about authority in the family and the role of women, both within the family and externally, in society. Her parents hold different values from each other, but her mother expresses her view to Veronica only secretly. Consider the differing impact the following statements would likely have on Veronica. Keep in mind that in her emotional state, she is especially vulnerable.

Example A

"Of course, the medical course must look very appealing, with this young man of yours taking a pre-med major. But let's look at what your father is saying, in a calmer frame of mind. After all, he is your father and the head of the family and he has always been there for you, hasn't he? Do you doubt his love for you?"

Example B

"How very painful for you all of this is. It seems as though your father has no regard for your right to choose your future. It must be hard for you that your mother is afraid to stand up to him openly."

Example C

"It's hard to make sense of this. You're just trying to choose the career you feel will be best for you. That's only what everyone else is doing. Of course, you feel angry and hurt."

Example D

"This must be really upsetting and confusing, trying to choose what you feel certain is the right path for you and getting such mixed signals from your parents, especially so much upset from your dad. I wonder if your mom and dad might each have different expectations for you, that even they can't agree on and don't talk about—either with you or each other. Let's talk about some ways we might go about sorting this out."

Of course, all counselors would like to believe that they would come up with the response in Example D. Indeed, we may even say these words to Veronica, but we must explore our underlying attitudes and beliefs so that we are not unconsciously giving Veronica the messages in Examples A, B, or C.

Example A shows how a counselor's paternalistic values can be expressed to influence Veronica to give in to her father and put away her ambition to become a pediatric oncologist. Veronica might even feel guilty and ashamed of her aspirations, but even if she is persuaded to give them up, much pain is likely to remain. However, she might be angered by the counselor's condescending attitude and his or her assumptions that her aspirations are merely a convenience to further her relationship with her boyfriend. Such an experience would probably confirm her negative attitude toward counseling; in this event she would be most unlikely to return for a further session.

A counselor might also offer an Example A response in an attempt to be culturally competent. He or she may assume from Veronica's last name that the family and Veronica are all steeped in Hispanic culture. Such a counselor also presumes to fully understand how to approach Veronica about her concerns. As Veronica is likely quickly to recognize the counselor's egregious error, it is highly likely she will react with anger and not return. Once again, she is likely to feel more depressed. Counseling, the resource that should be helpful to her, will instead look negative in her eyes.

By contrast, the counselor of Example B is expressing his or her own antimale views. In a sense, Veronica has been thinking much the same thoughts, but she has also been longing for resolution. The judgmental statements of this counselor indicate that the counselor's influence would be to tend to alienate Veronica from her father and possibly also from her mother. However, the possibility also exists that Veronica would not return for a second session because she would not have felt validated in all her complex feelings about her family—only in the current negative ones. In this case, she would probably feel even more depressed, but after such a negative experience, it is not likely that she would be willing to try counseling again.

The counselor of Example C shares values similar to Veronica's own. Veronica would most likely feel validated in her feelings with this counselor but frustrated in finding a resolution to the problem, as the counselor would be as blind as she herself is. Veronica might continue for some sessions but probably would drop out because her problem would continue unresolved. There would be risk, however, that she and the counselor would label her father as the villain in the family, creating an unnecessary distancing and hostility. In this situation, the counselor's apparent lack of multicultural knowledge, training, and sensitivity block the possibility of perceiving the difference in values that is key to helping Veronica cope with her family situation.

The counselor of Example D speaks entirely in the framework of values of Veronica and her family, validating Veronica without speaking against either of her parents. This counselor also immediately leads to opening a discussion in which differences of values and cultural views can be explored.

❧ Control of the Impact of the Counselor's Variables ❧

A plan for control of the impact of the counselor's values consists of the following steps. First, the counselor needs to be fully aware of his or her values. Multicultural training is extremely helpful in developing this awareness. Arredondo et al. (1996) stated that culturally skilled counselors "can recognize in a counseling or teaching relationship, when and how their attitudes, beliefs and values are interfering with providing the best service to clients" (p. 58) and as they are "able to recognize the limits of their competencies, they (a) seek consultation, (b) seek further training or education, (c) refer out to more qualified individuals or resources, or (d) engage in a combination of these" (p. 61).

Second, the counselor needs extensive training and knowledge in multicultural, career, and family counseling, in part to sharpen self-knowledge of values, in part to develop understanding and appreciation of other cultural values, and in part to build the body of knowledge needed to work with complex multicultural cases. In addition, not only does a counselor need to be knowledgeable of subcultures (in this case, Central American and Jewish), but he or she needs to also be sensitive to within-group differences that may occur.

As with Example A above, a counselor may be influenced by his or her limited knowledge of Latino families. Believing that Veronica was brought up in a traditional Latino home where the father has the last word in the family, this counselor might believe that his or her approach is a culturally sensitive approach. This counselor may not even be aware that the approach is inappropriate for this client and obviously would need more multicultural training and supervision to be able to recognize and plan for his or her negative impact on the client.

The third step of planning to control counselor values is to assess the values that are salient in each case and then determine which are at variance with the counselor's own values. When the counselor's values differ from the salient values in the case, it is the counselor's task to present neutrality of judgment and, always, advocacy for the client.

In Veronica's case, the effect of culture on gender roles might indeed be an issue, but the priority issue seems to be family communication and understanding. Unlike Counselor B, an experienced multicultural feminist therapist would be able to handle the salient values in Veronica's case in a way that is accepting of her lifestyle focal point. Such feminist therapists realize that for many clients gender may not be the most significant factor in their lives. Although the counselor may believe that it is important for Veronica to express her anger over the sexist attitudes of her father, the family and career factors of her case will be treated at the client's level of priority. In order for the counselor in Example B to be effective, he or she needs to be able to reach this level of expertise.

Counselor B may be unaware of his or her own feminist identity development issues and would benefit from counseling with an experienced feminist therapist on these issues before working with clients with similar issues, like Veronica. Arredondo et al. (1996) also pointed out the importance of knowing when a client needs to be referred to someone better qualified to work on the client's issues.

Both client and counselor bring their multiple perspectives and their differing lifestyle focal points into counseling, and it is therefore necessary when planning for interventions to have explored all of these factors in advance. When counselors find that their values differ from their clients, counselors must work to be consistently neutral. As part of the ongoing therapeutic work, it is often helpful to identify the value as a cultural variable. Equally important is that the counselor recognize when his or her values are too close to the client's to be helpful in getting the client to change, as in Example C. Again, if this is the case, the counselor should consider referring the client to someone else.

☙ Helpful Interventions ❧

To help Veronica with her dilemma, we attempt a solution-focused family approach to Donald Super's developmental career counseling (see chapter 3). Solution-focused therapy is a particularly appropriate choice for Veronica in view of her discomfort about seeing a counselor. This approach places emphasis on the problem rather than on the client per se. Because the client decides what her goals are and how she will know when she has achieved them, the solution-focused approach is also very empowering. Super's approach is used here because of its adaptability to multiple aspects of an individual's life.

The counselor's skills will be called on to help Veronica break down her goals into concrete, achievable steps and to ask the questions that enable her to work in the directions that lead her toward resolutions. It is likely, because of her lifestyle focal point, that Veronica may choose to attempt to reconcile her father to her choice of a career. A key to this goal is her clearer understanding and appreciation of her own Hispanic roots. This understanding will aid in future decision making in that she will be able to sort out the multiple roles she plays now and throughout her lifetime.

Session 1

In the first session, Veronica will establish several goals, which will probably include attending classes regularly (she was cutting class), working on family relationships in some way, making a final career decision, and possibly engaging in more social activity (she was withdrawn from friends). Simply by being able to set these clearly stated goals, she will begin to see the problem as finite and workable and will begin to feel empowered to work through her problem.

Before ending this first session, we might want to explore Veronica's values. She obviously values equality, her family, and her own ability and achievement. She needs to know how much of each of these and any other factors are driving her career decision. A brief period will be spent on values clarification so that Veronica has a better understanding of what is most important to her.

Veronica will have homework tasks to complete for the next session, perhaps the Salience Inventory and some exploratory reading in Hispanic culture, for example, *Harvest Empire: A History of Latinos in America* (Gonzalez, 2001) and *Strangers Among Us: Latino Lives in a Changing America (Suro, 1999)*. According to Super's (1957, 1984, 1992) theory of career maturity, Veronica is right on track—she is moving from a tentative career preference to a specific preference. More important to her now is an exploration of how her values and her chosen lifestyle will impact her career choice. The Salience Inventory (Nevil & Super, 1986) measures an individual's commitment to and participation in five major life roles: worker, student, citizen, homemaker, and leisurite. It will help Veronica understand more about the lifestyle she wants. The bibliotherapy assignment may also help her to understand more about her father's values regarding these same roles.

Session 2

We review Veronica's Salience Inventory and her understanding of her preferred lifestyle as well as the roles she finds to be most important. At present, Veronica sees work as her most important role but foresees that home and family will be equally important to her in the future. With this understanding, we can turn the focus to her bicultural roots and how they shape her parents' relationship to each other, their gender roles and expectations, and their differing expectations of her.

Veronica's reading on Latino culture will give her knowledge of her father's background. She will, most likely, learn about gender roles in Latino families, specifically, *machismo*—the essence of being a man and having self-respect and the responsibility for protecting and providing for the family. Perhaps this knowledge will help Veronica to see her father as trying to be a good Latino dad. She would be asked how this shifts her perception of his views about her choice of major and what ideas it gives her about how to talk to him about her career choice.

As we talk, it will become clear that there is much family history on both sides that she might like to know more about. This is an opportunity to introduce the idea of a genogram. To explain how one is done, refer to a source of help (Dunn & Levitt, 2000; McGoldrick, Gerson, & Shellenberger, 1999) and encourage her to call, write, and visit relatives. Because her mother also has not continued her own cultural heritage, this is an exciting, enriching venture into her cultural roots on both sides of her family.

Session 3

The third session is delayed to give Veronica time to pursue her homework. Because she is again attending classes and socializing to a reasonable degree, the delay was considered acceptable. Veronica comes to the third session animated by her interest in the family background on both sides, although there is much more to do. She has still been avoiding contact with her parents since their last visit, although she has not yet taken steps to change her major. She wants to see her father and get back on good terms with him, but she feels very uncertain about his attitude toward her.

When asked how this avoidance behavior is helping her to achieve her goal of improving relationships, Veronica says that it is keeping them from arguing because she still feels unwilling to give up her career choice. Veronica does not think her father would be willing to come to a session with her. She uses the session to talk about what she wants to say to him and how best to say it. When Veronica thinks of a point that she believes will start another argument rather than productive conversation, she is encouraged to write, read, and burn those thoughts.

Veronica believes her father is anxious for her to marry and have children and that she can reassure him about that. Her fear is that her father's reluctance to support her medical school plans is based on a cultural belief that if she is married, she must be the dutiful wife and a mother who puts the family first. Veronica, however, believes she will be able to manage both family and career, and doing both is important to her. Veronica considers being unable to get her father's approval the worst-case scenario that could happen, but she is beginning to think that she would be able to handle that too. She will need to make alternative plans for supporting herself in medical school, and she will continue to strive to get her father to accept her decision.

Session 4

Veronica is still attending classes and socializing but is temporizing about changing her major or going to see her father, although since the last session she is feeling somewhat more optimistic about it. She will be asked what is working or what is she doing that is helping her get closer to reaching her goal. She is likely to admit that she is staying with her decision to go to medical school and feels stronger in her defense of that decision. She also believes she knows more about why her father might be against it. She would like her mother to come to a session and believes her mother would attend a session with her. We do not wish to ask her mother to come alone, as such a session would support the triangulation her mother has already initiated. Nor do we wish to invite both parents to attend with Veronica, believing that the risk to our client outweighs the likelihood of success. If Veronica's mother is unwilling to support her openly, one family session in solution-focused therapy is unlikely to change the dynamic supporting the secret. This decision can be reconsidered later, if Veronica does well with her father and he withdraws his disapproval of her career choice. We ask Veronica how she believes meeting with her mother will help us forward her situation with her father. Using this question to bring focus back to her goal helps her to decide that such a meeting would not be helpful.

We give another homework assignment: to apply her father's life to the career rainbow to get an understanding of the multiple roles he must play, which roles are the ones he feels are most important, and how culture has influenced the values he places on those roles. Finally, using this new understanding of his perspective, Veronica is asked to rehearse how she will ask her father for what she wants.

Session 5

Veronica reports at the last session that she did visit with her father alone, and though the visit did not go as well as she hoped, she felt it was promising. At least they were back on good terms, and he was pleased about her boyfriend and looking forward to meeting his family. They were also planning a trip to see her grandmother in San Francisco together, and Veronica was excited about that. She was thinking about taking Spanish classes also. In this session, we explore the possible meanings of her mother's need for secrecy. If her mother is triangulating with her out of a family dynamic, we can help Veronica to have some understanding and ability to cope with that behavior, although she may need to return to counseling at a later time about it. Veronica's last assignment is to research some possible sources of scholarships and low-interest loans for her medical school education. Veronica is congratulated on her hard, courageous, and successful work throughout the counseling, and the door is left open for further sessions as needed.

With this approach, Veronica has a high chance of maintaining a good relationship with her father, even if he decides not to finance her medical school. Veronica is also developing an enriched understanding and appreciation of her bicultural roots and perhaps, if she chooses, contact and friendships with relatives completely new to her. Finally, she has had a successful experience with the resource of counseling that may be useful to her or members of her family at some future points of her life.

༄ Summary ๏๕

The needs of this client necessitated an application of both family and career counseling theories. Had we focused only on career issues and looked at Veronica as an individual regardless of context, we would have been doing a disservice to our client. Had we only focused on family issues, Veronica's career issues may have been, at best, minimized, and at worst, ignored. The integration of these approaches works with this client primarily because the counselors felt comfortable working out of their respective boxes of family and career counseling.

༄ References ๏๕

Arredondo, P., Toporek, R., Brown, S. P., Jones, J., Locke, D. C., Sanchez, J., & Stadler, H. (1996). Operationalization of the multicultural counseling competencies. *Journal of Multicultural Counseling and Development, 24,* 42-78.

Dunn, A. B., & Levitt, M. M. (2000). The genogram: From diagnostics to mutual collaboration. *Family Journal of Counseling and Therapy for Couples and Families, 8,* 236-244.

Gonzalez, J. (2001). *Harvest of empire: A history of Latinos in America.* New York: Penguin.

McGoldrick, M., Gerson, R., & Shellenberger, S. (1999). *Genograms: Assessment and intervention* (2nd ed.). New York: Norton.

Nevil, D. D., & Super, D. E. (1986). *The salience inventory.* Palo Alto, CA: Consulting Psychologists Press.

Okun, B. F. (1996). *Understanding diverse families: What practitioners need to know.* New York: Guilford Press.

Super, D. E. (1957). *The psychology of careers.* New York: Harper & Row.

Super, D. E. (1984). Career and life development. In D. Brown, L. Brooks, & Associates (Eds.), *Career choice development: Applying contemporary theories to practice* (pp. 192-234). San Francisco: Jossey-Bass.

Super, D. E. (1992). Toward a comprehensive theory of career development. In D. H. Montross & C. J. Shinkman (Eds.), *Career development: Theory and practice* (pp. 35-64). Springfield, IL: Charles C. Thomas.

Suro, R. (1999). *Strangers among us: Latino lives in a changing America.* New York: Vintage Books.

♱ Chapter 5 ♱

Strategies for Counseling Family Two:
The Rokutani Family

Kim Snow and Jon Carlson

Yuri is a 32-year-old woman native to Japan. She married her husband, Jonathon, a yonsei—a fourth-generation Japanese and the third generation born in the United States. Five years ago, Jonathon was sent by his company to work in their office in Japan. There he met Yuri, who was working in the company offices. After a 2-year courtship, they married in a traditional Buddhist ceremony, much to his parent's dismay, because Jonathon is Catholic. They continued to work in the office in Japan for 3 more years until Jonathon was transferred back to the United States. Although Yuri was not pleased to leave her family behind, she followed her husband. Unfortunately, she had to leave her position in the company and was not guaranteed employment in the United States.

They now reside in a small midwestern town with a limited Asian population and only one other family of Japanese descent. They are expecting their first child in 4 months. Since returning to the United States, Yuri has entered graduate school and is working part time as a research assistant at the local university. Although Jonathon is advancing in his career, Yuri is feeling the pressure to take responsibility for her forthcoming child while at the same time continue on her career path.

In addition, Yuri has found that her limited English language skills, cultural and religious differences, and the absence of an extended family support system have created a gulf between her and Jonathon. Yuri is very anxious about the situation and has bouts of depression. Jonathon is becoming impatient with the difficulties she is having, because he felt that he was able to assimilate during his 5 years in Japan.

This chapter is dedicated to Dr. Burt Collins, a respected and beloved colleague, whose untimely death prevented him from writing this chapter. Our thoughts go out to him and his family.

When one reads about the above scenario, it is very common to view this family's problem in the context of family problems or vocational issues or from a multicultural perspective, depending on what theoretical orientation the counselor chooses. Although any one of these views can help the family to some degree, if we were to look at the family from a single perspective, it would be a very limited view of this particular family. To work with Yuri and Jonathon in the most beneficial way requires an integration of these three orientations and approaches to counseling. This means, in other words, looking at the family's situation from the multidimensional lens of a multicultural counselor, a family counselor, *and* a career counselor rather than a one-dimensional approach to a multidimensional problem.

The different factors that are affecting Yuri and Jonathon's relationship can be viewed within the framework of the hourglass model that is illustrated in chapter 2. The lifestyle focal points for the Rokutani family at this current time are the issues surrounding family, career, culture, and gender and need to be the focus of the counseling. As mentioned in chapter 2, there are multiple variables such as Yuri and Jonathon's age, race, sexual orientation, physical and intellectual abilities, income, values, ethnicity, religion, traditions, education, interests, and personality that all influence Yuri and Jonathon's constructs of family, career, culture, and gender. These variables do need to be looked at by the counselor and addressed within the context of the lifestyle focal points.

For example, when exploring what the concept of family means to Yuri and Jonathon, the counselor can expect differing views. This family is dealing with two differing and somewhat opposing concepts of what a family is and what a family means for each of them. Yuri identifies with the traditional Japanese model of family, and Jonathon is more familiar with the Western or American ideas of what a family is. Yuri and Jonathon's different values, religions, ethnicity, and traditions have all shaped how each of them identifies what family means to them personally. It will be the counselor's task not only to help Yuri and Jonathon become aware of how their different backgrounds and histories have shaped their ideas and ideals about family but also to help Yuri and Jonathon to respect and honor their similarities and differences so that together they can forge their own path of what their family will look like—a blending of the two cultures, histories, and traditions. This is particularly important when one also identifies the developmental stage of this family. Jonathon and Yuri are expecting their first child in 4 months. If they can learn to integrate and understand how their values, ethnicity, religion, traditions, education, and interests will impact how they want to be as parents and how they want to raise their child, Yuri and Jonathon will have a stronger, more united foundation of family to stand on as they embark on their journey as parents.

Culture is another lifestyle focal point for Jonathon and Yuri at this particular time. Although both Yuri and Jonathon share a common Japanese heritage, their culture is very different. Yuri is an *issei*, or first-generation Japanese who was raised in a traditional Japanese culture, whereas Jonathon is a *yonsei*, a fourth-generation Japanese American who grew up in a very Westernized American culture. Not only were Yuri and Jonathon raised in two very different cultures, but they each have very different acculturation rates. Because Jonathon was able to adapt to the Japanese culture when he lived in Japan, he is not very understanding of the difficulty that Yuri is experiencing since moving to the United States.

Another major focal point for Yuri and Jonathon is career. Jonathon's career appears to be very bright and climbing steadily. Yuri's career is taking a backseat to Jonathon's since she had to give up her job and relocate because of his job. Another area of contention for Yuri and Jonathon will be how to integrate child-care and parenting issues with each of their careers. This also leads to the final focal point, which is gender issues. How does the traditional Japanese role of men and women that Yuri holds fit with Jonathon's Americanized expectations? How are Jonathon and Yuri's messages about gender affected by living in the United States at the current time?

As we can see, there are multiple issues that Yuri and Jonathon are bringing to the counseling arena. Not only does the counselor have to deal with the above mentioned lifestyle focal points that Yuri and Jonathon are presenting with, but the counselor needs to also address the impact of all of the variables mentioned in the hourglass conceptualization, as explained in chapter 2. Although, each of these variables is discussed in greater detail throughout this chapter, it is important to keep in mind how they all interplay and can be viewed within the framework of the hourglass model.

As proposed by Beutell and Berman (1999), life satisfaction is the result of a combination of family, job, and career satisfaction. Each component of work, family, and one's cultural background is interdependent, with each domain having an impact on the other areas (Forest, 1994; Jones & Fletcher, 1993). If one role of life (whether it be family or career) is out of balance or has changed, it affects the other areas. For example, a husband's new job will have an impact on the family because the family may have to move, the husband may have to work different hours, the new job may change the family's income, and the husband may have to give more attention to the job (and less to family matters) as he accommodates to the new responsibilities. This results in more of the household and family responsibilities for the wife to deal with. This chapter examines each of the factors mentioned in the hourglass figure that is affecting Yuri's and Jonathon's lives while still maintaining a view of the macrosystem, or larger picture.

੭ Understanding the Client's Worldview ੬

It is crucial for the counselor to gain an understanding of the clients' worldview. Yuri and Jonathon bring many complex issues into the counseling arena. Here we have two clients with varying worldviews. Not only do we as counselors need to understand where each is coming from, but we also need to understand that part of their communication difficulty is that Jonathon does not understand his wife's worldview. To tailor the therapy for this specific couple and to address all of the complexities of this case, it is important to look at each aspect of the model presented in Chapter 2.

Family

When working with families, it is essential for the counselor to have an understanding of how culture affects the families' lifestyle. "Family" has a different meaning for each culture. For example, it is common for Asian Americans' sense of family to also encompass the extended family, and very often a lineage of ancestry. For Asian Americans, the family is seen as the central unit, with the individual being secondary (Goldenberg & Goldenberg, 1998). Asian families generally focus on ideals such as interdependence, honor, and community, whereas the American or Westernized culture generally promotes more of a nuclear family system in which independence and individualism are stressed. It is of utmost importance that the counselor explores how this Asian American family has integrated (or is struggling) with these dichotomous views of family. Has Jonathon adopted the Western perception of family with its emphasis on individualism and independence? How does this fit with Yuri's traditional Japanese view of family that encompasses the extended family and encourages such ideals as interdependence and community? Can this family assimilate these contradicting beliefs about family in a way that honors each individual and both cultures within this family?

Yuri and Jonathon have been married for approximately 3 years. As mentioned in the case presentation, Yuri is expecting a child within 4 months. Their family life cycle is undergoing the transition from newly weds in a marital dyad where the focus was on their respective roles as wife and husband into the new, foreign territory of an "infant family" where Yuri and Jonathon both have to learn the roles of new parents while still maintaining their familiar roles as spouses and career-minded individuals. Typically in families, there is a transition and adjustment period during which the marital relationship is strained while the primary focus of attention becomes the new child and adjusting to the responsibilities of parenting.

This developmental scenario takes on further complexities when working with Asian American families because, in many traditional Asian families, the dominant relationship within these families often focuses on the parent–child dyad rather than the relationship between husband and wife. In many cases, as described by Lee (1996), "the strongest emotional attachment for a woman is sometimes, not her husband, but her children (especially her sons)" (p. 231). Depending on how "Westernized" or acculturated Jonathon is, this could have several implications. If he is Americanized and views the marital dyad as the primary relationship within the family, he could feel very displaced as Yuri focuses most of her attentions on the new child. If Jonathon takes the traditional Japanese role of provider and disciplinarian, and Yuri assumes the traditional Asian role of mother, they may find that many of their relationship issues become less significant as Yuri becomes more involved in the relationship with her new child and less involved with her husband. He may have his career and she may have the child as a primary relationship.

New milestones in family development, such as becoming parents for the first time, can be a stressful time for any family, and usually families do depend on the support of their extended families or families of origin. Japanese extended families tend to be very involved in the raising of children. As mentioned by Lee (1996), it is common for children to be raised not only by their parents but also by a wide range of adults (grandparents, uncles, aunts, cousins, wet nurses, and older siblings). Yuri and Jonathon appear to have no extended family support in close proximity. It is important that the counselor explores the lack of extended family support with Yuri and Jonathon. How are Yuri and Jonathon coping with the lack of support? Can one of the grandmothers (or another family member) come to visit and help with the newborn child? Is there any local support? What are Yuri and Jonathon's expectations, and how can their needs be accommodated within the community where they are living?

In addition to the lack of familial support, Yuri has to contend with the cultural differences in health care and traditions. Prenatal care and childbirth practices are different in Japan and the United States. These changes will be further heightened when the couple addresses issues such as child-care and child-rearing practices. For example, will the baby be raised from the tradition of a Japanese perspective or from a more Americanized perspective? And, how comfortable are the parents with their choices and those of the other partner? How will the couple's religious differences be integrated into their new family? Will the child be raised as a Catholic or a Buddhist? And, how much are their choices determined (or limited) by the community that they now live in? Is there a Buddhist temple within the small midwestern town?

Career

This family has been a dual-career family with the primary focus on Jonathon's career and their move to the United States. It would be advantageous to explore what type of dual-career marriage Yuri and Jonathon possess. Seligman (1994) identified three types of dual-career marriages: *traditional* (in which the wife is expected to bear the responsibility for the family and housekeeping), *participant* (in which the husband is partially involved in the household and family responsibilities but his contribution is viewed as helping rather than sharing), and *role sharing* (in which both the husband and wife are actively involved in the household duties and child care). It would be helpful to address these various types of dual-career options and ascertain if Yuri and Jonathon have similar expectations about their roles as a dual-career family. From the case study presented, it is evident that there has been many recent changes for Jonathon and Yuri that have affected both of their careers.

Jonathon has been working for the same company for several years. He was transferred to Japan with this job and then 5 years later was relocated back to the United States. It appears as though Jonathon's career is going well and he is advancing within the company.

Jonathon appears to be in the early middle adult years of his career (28–35 years of age). Cox (1970) found that career development and success are of considerable importance to adults within this age group and that there appears to be a strong correlation between an individual's mental health and feelings of self-actualization and accomplishment through one's career. According to Levinson (1986), this is typically a period of deep growth and productivity within family relationships and careers. There are several milestones that are also accomplished during this phase of life, which include people establishing themselves within their community and society, starting and raising families, and moving ahead in their chosen vocations. These rites of passage are also a time of great energy, accomplishment, and stress. Some avenues that a counselor may want to explore with Jonathon might include addressing many of the stressors that are also prevalent among career-minded adults of this age cohort, such as the interactions and balancing of individual, family, career demands, having and rearing children, dealing with aging parents and obligations to the older generation, and the general responsibilities of adulthood. Jonathon's career history and his individual and career goals are worth exploring in the counseling process.

Yuri and Jonathon currently live in a small Midwest town with limited exposure to other Japanese American or Asian American families. As noted by several researchers (Anderson & Apostle, 1971; Sewell &

Orenstein, 1965), environmental factors can play a large part in influ-encing and determining career paths and choices. People from small towns and residing in small towns tend to have limited occupational information and a restricted range of opportunities available to them (Seligman, 1994). This is especially significant for Yuri because she has several career issues that she is dealing with. She gave up her position in Japan as an office worker and followed her husband to the United States. It appears as though Yuri was quite stable in her job at the office in Japan because she had been working there for a number of years. As is customary in Asian cultures, she gave up her personal ambitions (her individual wishes and desires) for the collective good of the family (to be an obedient, dutiful wife). Yuri was also not guaranteed a job in the United States. Since moving to the United States, she recently entered graduate school and is working part time as a research assistant. It was also revealed that Yuri speaks limited English, which will limit her abil-ity to get another job in the local area. The fact that she is soon expect-ing their first child will further impact Yuri's career choices and possibilities. An area that definitely needs to be taken into consideration is how child care and parenting will affect both of their careers. Do they both have similar expectations of each other? How do they feel about working mothers? Are their views compatible? And, who will stay home from work when the child is sick?

As is evidenced from the details we know about Yuri, she has under-gone a lot of recent losses in her life for which there will be a multitude of grief issues. She had to leave her family, her country, and her job to be a dutiful wife and follow her husband back to the United States for his job. Yuri is also adjusting to a lot of new changes. She is adjusting to a new culture (American) with limited Japanese contact, she has a new part-time job as a research assistant that is very different from her for-mer job as an office worker, she has started graduate school, and she is soon to be a mother. Yuri is already feeling the pressure to care for her forthcoming child (without family support) while continuing her career path. From the case presentation, it appears as though Jonathon is advancing in his career and has little time to support Yuri or nurture their relationship. Also uncertain is the support and commitment that he will be able to provide in regard to the demands of a newborn.

Different Backgrounds and Cultures

Although both Yuri and Jonathon are of Japanese descent, they have very different backgrounds, cultures, and levels of acculturation. This is further delineated by the fact that Japanese Americans have a distinct numbering system for each of the succeeding generations of Japanese who have migrated to the United States (Matsui, 1996). As mentioned in the case presentation, Jonathon is a yonsei (a fourth-generation Japanese and the third generation to be born in the United States). Jonathon has become acculturated to the American way of life. His integration into the American lifestyle is evident by his "American" or Westernized name and his Catholic religion. It appears as though his family through the generations and acculturation has rejected some of their Japanese heritage and culture and adopted a more Americanized lifestyle and identity.

Yuri is an issei (a first-generation immigrant). Until she moved to the United States, Yuri had no experience outside her own culture, being born and raised in Japan. From what we know about Yuri, it appears that she really had no contact with any cultures other than her traditional Japanese upbringing. This is also congruent with Yuri's limited capacity to speak English. Her poor language skills, her unfamiliarity with the American (Midwest) culture, and her traditional upbringing will affect her ability to adapt to the Western culture as easily as Jonathon.

Lee (1996) described these varying levels of acculturation within a family as a *culture-conflict family* in which struggles not only occur because of the differing levels of acculturation but are exasperated by differences in such areas as religion, philosophy, and politics. This is evidenced by their contrasting religious beliefs. Jonathon was raised as a Catholic, whereas Yuri had a traditional Buddhist indoctrination. Though they were married in a traditional Buddhist marriage ceremony, it appears that there was a split in the family's acceptance of those differences. Jonathan's Catholic family appears not to have approved of the Buddhist wedding ceremony.

There is a growing schism between Yuri and Jonathon in regard to her limited acculturation to the American way of life. It seems that Jonathon is not very supportive of Yuri's loneliness—her isolation from her extended family, her cultural and religious barriers, and her limited English language skills. This cultural schism appears to be heightened by the communication difficulties Yuri is facing. The distorted communication is exacerbating Yuri's bouts of depression and feelings of anxiety concerning her current living situation. Jonathon contributes to the problem by not being very understanding or accepting of her difficulties; since he was able to adapt to life in Japan, he expects Yuri to react the same way that he did when he found himself living in a foreign country.

As we work with this couple, it would be important to have each of them understand where the other is coming from. This would entail some couple's work whereby the counselor ensures that both parties feel heard and understood. By teaching Yuri and Johnathon how to listen to one another and to really hear where the other is coming from, we can then help them work toward establishing some common ground and building a stronger foundation of communication.

Gender

It is also important to look at the role that gender plays within Yuri and Jonathon's family. From their different backgrounds and levels of acculturation, we can assume that both Yuri and Jonathon will have some different perceptions of the role of a husband and wife as well as their roles as parents. It would be valuable to find out what their individual views are on the role of husband and wife and as parents because of their different levels of acculturation. Do they have similar perceptions of their roles as a husband and a wife? How will their perceptions of being a husband or wife and of being a family be affected by living in the United States?

Socioeconomic Status

Jonathon is a professional and Yuri was an office worker when they first met. Since relocating to the United States, Yuri is now going to graduate school and is a research assistant. Yuri has had to adapt not only to living in a different culture but also to living in a higher socioeconomic strata than she formally did in Japan. Although the higher economic level may open some choices to Yuri, there will also be obstacles that she may confront. One key difference that will certainly have an impact on their lifestyle is the focus on material things. Yuri, being raised as a traditional Buddhist, would not place a high value on things; however, Jonathon, as a fourth-generation Japanese American, would place more value in materialism and acquiring things, as most Americans do.

The impending child will also have a socioeconomic impact on this couple. Can Yuri choose to stay home if she wanted to raise the child? Does she need to work? How does Jonathon feel about her being a working mother? How does Yuri feel about it in respect to her traditional upbringing?

Society

As mentioned in the case summary, it appears as though Yuri and Jonathon are culturally isolated without much local support, religious support, or cultural traditions and community. Both Yuri and Jonathon are currently located in a small midwestern town with a limited Asian population and only one other family of Japanese descent. Yuri's modest language skills will probably place further limits on the community support because there are not many people around who can converse with her. Lee (1996) addressed Yuri's situation specifically when he warned that those who live in rural or small towns with relatively isolated Asian populations generally have more trouble adjusting and feel pressured to assimilate more quickly (McGoldrick, Giordano, & Pierce, 1996). This cultural isolation and the stresses of migration that Yuri is feeling need to be addressed in counseling. Some of the avenues that a counselor should explore with Yuri and Jonathon include the effects of racism, prejudice, and discrimination that they experience within their new environment. And, is it possible for the family to have closer relations with Jonathon's family?

As we can see from the presenting case and the breakdown of the various factors that affect Yuri and Jonathon, this is a complex case with many interlaced and interdependent issues. Analyzing all of the aspects that affect Yuri and Jonathon help us to comprehend just how important it is to address this case from a multidimensional, holistic approach rather than using a surface application of strictly a family counselor, a career counselor, or a multicultural counselor.

৯> Understanding Asian Americans and How They View Mental Health ৎ১

Just as it is paramount that counselors understand the powerful roles that ethnicity, race, and culture play within their own lives, when working with a Japanese American family such as Yuri and Jonathon, it is critical for counselors to have an understanding of the Asian American population and how counseling is viewed by this culture. Asian Americans have often been viewed as a "model minority" by contemporary society (S. Sue & Sue, 1990). Japanese and Chinese Americans, in particular, are often depicted as successful and well adapted because of their economic and educational attainment (Lee, 1996; Sandhu, 1997; D. W. Sue, 1990). Although this successful view of Asian Americans is widely accepted, a more in-depth analysis reveals a very different side to the success stories that are depicted in the popular media. Although census figures document that high-achieving Asian Americans do tend to have a higher median income and education level, it does not take into account the diversity and the wide range of group variance within the Asian American population. The reality is that, as a group, Asian Americans reveal a bimodal distribution made up of the visible, highly successful, professional group and a group of recent immigrants and refugees with little education, low economic status, poor living conditions, and much less success (S. Sue & Sue, 1990).

As mentioned by Carlson and Carlson (2000), the stigmatization of Asian American as the model and successful minority has created a false illusion that Asian Americans are somehow immune or unaffected by the negative forces of prejudice and discrimination. They are seen as a well-adjusted minority group that functions effectively in society and experiences few difficulties or psychological problems (Lee, 1996). This stereotype of a prosperous, well-adapted minority is further perpetuated by the underutilization of mental health services by Asian Americans. Behind the successful facade of many Asian Americans, the facts reveal a much starker view of reality. Available research reveals that Asian Americans have a rate of psychopathology and depression equal to or higher than European Americans (Kuo, 1984; Uba, 1994). As reported by S. Sue and Sue (1990), much of the mental illness, the adjustment difficulties, and the juvenile delinquency among Asian Americans are hidden. Research suggests that the underutilization of psychological and psychiatric services is attributable to "such cultural factors as the shame and disgrace with admitting emotional problems, the handling of problems within the family rather than relying on outside resources, and the manner of symptom formation, such as low acting-out disorders" (S. Sue & Sue, 1990, p. 192).

It is also important to note that many Asian clients tend to express their emotional pain in terms of somatic physical complaints and metaphoric language. Tanaka (1979) revealed the significance of addressing cultural implications when dealing with mental health issues. The word association surrounding depression (yuutsu) was compared among the Japanese culture and that of Western Americans. Tanaka discovered that the Japanese made concrete external and environmental associations to depression, such as rain, clouds, headache, fatigue, and darkness, whereas the Western Americans tended to describe depression with internally negatively associated mood states, such sadness, loneliness, and being down.

The above information stresses the significance of cultural sensitivity when dealing with a family such as Yuri and Jonathon. This is especially important when the counselor is non–Asian American. Because of the varying degrees of acculturation, Jonathon may be more "Americanized" in his thinking, but since Yuri is more "traditional," she would likely be very inhibited in presenting for counseling because of the strong cultural prohibitions against the admission of personal problems and the shame that it brings on the individual and the entire family. It would also be crucial for the counselor not only to explore Yuri's emotional distress but also to assess her physical health because many Asians tend to express their psychological pain in somatic terms.

Another important factor to consider when working with Jonathon and Yuri is that typically Japanese American families tend to not be very receptive to the counseling process. Nevertheless, Asian Americans do tend to be more receptive to career counseling than many other ethnic groups (Leong, 1985). This information may be used to encourage Yuri and Jonathon to commit to counseling. If we begin by focusing on the career and the impact that family discord and individual stress have on the careers as well as the impact on the family, we may have better luck retaining this couple in counseling.

❦ Impact of Counselor Variables ❦

When working with any client, it is paramount that counselors understand the powerful roles that ethnicity, race, and culture play within their own lives as well as the lives of the people with whom they work. Are there barriers that the counselors bring from their own cultural upbringing that could hinder them from working effectively with Yuri and Jonathon? Counselors typically do most of their work through talk therapy, but if Yuri is hindered in her ability to effectively verbalize her feelings and thoughts because of language barriers and cultural upbringing, will this place her at a disadvantage in typical (in the box) therapy? Will the counselor be more aligned to Jonathon because of their commonalities, since Jonathon is more Americanized and able to speak fluent English? What precautions can the counselor take to prevent this from happening and to be aware of his or her own cultural biases?

Another culturally bound issue that needs to be taken into consideration is the delivery of services. The counselor may attempt to be forward, friendly, and informal as a way to relax the clients and build therapeutic rapport; however, such forward and informal behavior may be viewed by many Asian clients as disrespectful and threatening.

Many counselors unconsciously expect the culturally diverse clients to adapt to the counselor's (or mainstream society's) culture and values rather than the counselor accommodating to the values and culture of the client. This often leads to premature termination of clients and traditional mental health services (which are typically based on middle- to upper-class White values) being imposed on those clients who do choose to remain in therapy. Thus, it is critical that counselors have an awareness of their own cultural values and how these values can be imposed on others if the counselor is not aware of cultural barriers. It is of utmost importance that counselors meet each client where he or she is at, regardless of differences in cultural background. Once we as counselors have a clear understanding of our own cultural values and upbringing, and those of our clients, we can begin to tailor the therapy for the clients and work in the best interests of all clients.

❦ Working With Asian American Families From an Adlerian Stance ❦

Adlerian therapy is based on a holistic, growth model that is versatile in working with a diverse range of clients. Adlerian therapy is actually a technical eclectic approach (allowing therapists the freedom of apply-ing a variety of experiential, behavioral, and cognitive techniques) and can be useful in a wide range of areas, such as marital counseling, fam-ily therapy, parent–child counseling, child guidance, cultural conflicts, individual and group counseling, and vocational counseling (Watts, 1999). Pedersen (1990) described this approach as a culture-centered or a multicultural approach to counseling because of the sensitivity and the precedence given to cultural and gender issues (Corey, 2001). The wide application of Adlerian psychotherapy, combined with its adapt-ability and holistic nature, allows for a comprehensive and integrative way to work with a couple such as Yuri and Jonathon. This approach respects their individuality as well as their culture.

Tailoring Therapy

When working with a culturally diverse client, it is important to assess the client intrapersonally as well as interpersonally from the larger con-text of his or her cultural identity. This involves understanding the macro view of the client's world (his or her ethnicity and cultural background) while still maintaining a balance with the micro view of the client's identity. As purported by Berg and Miller (1992), counselors have to maintain a balance of the impact of culture on the client's worldview with how clients personally experience ethnic and cultural influences.

Adlerian psychotherapy focuses on the client *within* his or her social context. The Adlerian counselor values the subjective world of the client and attends to the acculturation and racial identity within the client's lifestyle (Carlson & Carlson, 2000). Viewing the client from a sub-jective frame of reference while still appreciating the larger social per-spective creates a tailoring of the therapeutic process for each client.

Although the name implies "individual" psychology, in reality, Adlerian therapy complements the integrative model of psychotherapy. This approach is based on the premise that there are five universal life tasks that all people must face and master (Dreikurs & Mosak, 1966, 1967): (a) relating to others (friendship and culture), (b) making a con-tribution (work), (c) achieving intimacy (love and family relationships), (d) getting along with ourselves (self-acceptance), and (e) developing our spiritual dimension (including values, meaning, life goals, and our relationship with the universe, or cosmos). Each of these areas are explored through the therapeutic process and would address all of the issues that Yuri and Jonathon are facing.

The therapeutic process is broken down into the following four phases (Dreikurs & Mosak, 1967): (a) establishing the therapeutic rela-tionship, (b) exploring the psychological dynamics operating within the clients (the assessment stage), (c) encouraging the development of self-understanding (insight into purpose), and (d) helping the client make new choices (reorientation and education). We discuss these phases next.

Establishing the Therapeutic Relationship. This initial phase of counseling involves building a collaborative, harmonious, interpersonal relationship that is based on trust, caring, mutual respect, interdependence, and a mutual obligation for creating harmony and peace (Carlson & Carlson, 2000). These concepts are based on such values as cooperation and socially oriented values that tend to be very aligned with those values of Asian American families.

Because many minorities are unfamiliar with the therapeutic process, it is important that the counselor explain his or her role and the process of counseling. This is also a good time for the counselor to establish a social or cultural connection by addressing the client's culture and sharing his or her experience (or lack of experience) with working with Asian American clients. During the initial session, the counselor should address the family in a formal and polite manner that respects and honors the client's cultural background and values.

One of the aspects of building a therapeutic relationship involves building on the client's strengths and assets. This encouragement is fostered by empathic listening, being authentic, caring for and respecting the client, and an underlying belief in the client's ability to grow and change. Many Asian Americans tend to have difficulty sharing personal or family problems or discussing psychological difficulties. This supportive environment tends to build a client's self-concept and self-respect that encourages the client to open up. This is particularly important with Asian American clients because therapy may often be associated with shame and disrespect.

Understanding the client's subjective worldview is the core element of this phase of therapy. The therapist attempts to grasp the nonverbal and verbal cues from the client, while looking for fundamental patterns and beliefs within the client's frame of reference. Adlerian counselors work with clients in a collaborative, respectful manner that takes the client's cultural values into account, enabling the client to reach his or her own self-defined goals. When working with an Asian American client or family, counselors need to realize that Asian Americans tend to prefer more tangible, specific goals. More complex goals are best broken down into a series of understandable, achievable, short-term goals that the client can see and can attain progress (Lee, 1996).

Exploring the Client's Dynamics: Assessment Phase. The second phase of counseling is often called the assessment phase because it is derived from two distinctive interviews: the subjective interview and the objective interview. The subjective interview involves the clients revealing their life history. This account of the clients' life provides the counselor with key information about how the clients view life and choose to cope with problems, as well as some of their concerns.

It is important to note that Asian Americans have been raised to respect their family heritage and are not comfortable with revealing detailed personal information about their families. They may question what this has to do with the problem at hand. The counselor needs to demonstrate sensitivity and understanding about the client's cultural background and values, and to explain the purpose of the interview and how it can help the client.

The objective interview seeks to uncover specific information regarding (a) how the client perceives the problems and his or her life (including how his or her cultural or religious beliefs view the cause of the problem); (b) any precipitating events; (c) a medical history, including current and past medications (and any somatic or physical symptoms); (d) a comprehensive account of the social support and interactions of the client; (e) the presenting problem; (f) the person's coping skills and strengths; (g) lifestyle assessment (a probing into the client's early childhood history and his or her family constellation). These comprehensive assessments are congruent to those proposed by many multicultural counselors. McGoldrick et al. (1996) illustrated the benefits of a holistic model in assessment and data collection when deal-ing with Asian American families. Their suggested model includes "(1) assessing the internal family system, which includes gaining an under-standing of the individual members and the family subsystems; and (2) assessing the external factors, which would include the impact of com-munity and other environmental stressors" (Lee, 1996, p. 234). Since Yuri and Jonathon have also experienced significant social change and cul-tural transition, gathering data such as the impact of cultural shock, racism, employment, and their recent move to a small Midwest commu-nity also should be taken into consideration.

These comprehensive assessments culminate in an integrated sum-mary. This summary is specifically tailored according to the client and generally provides a detailed narration of the client's subjective experi-ence and life story. This often includes a summary of early recollec-tions, the client's family constellation, his or her personal and cultural strengths and assets, some basic mistakes that the client may hold that interfere with the client's growth and goals, and a summary of coping strategies. The counselor and client then refine these summaries into more directive, specific points for the client to work on. Once again, the counselor should focus on refining these summaries into tangible spe-cific goals that are problem-focused and symptom-relieving.

Encouraging Self-Understanding and Insight. This phase involves the counselor making disclosures and interpretations that facilitate the clients' awareness of patterns of behavior, insight into goals and purposes, private logic (how the world is perceived), and current behavior. The counselor makes these interpretations in a manner that is nonthreatening and open-ended. This process encourages the clients to come to understand their motivations, ways that they are perpetuating the problems, and how they can choose to change their behavior.

Reorientation and Education. The action-oriented phase of therapy is the problem-solving and decision-making process. Reorientation and education is a phase that encourages clients to put their goals into action. Through the use of a variety of techniques, including immediacy, advice, humor, silence, acting as if, catching oneself, early recollection analysis, task setting, homework, and many others (Carlson & Slavich, 1997), clients are encouraged to recognize their personal power and to make holistic changes that will help them to gain more awareness about themselves, their family, and society, as well as to see new alternatives and make better choices.

❧ Helpful Interventions ❦

Applying Adlerian Therapy to Yuri and Jonathon

This case example is illustrated from the perspective of a male Caucasian counselor with little knowledge of Japanese or Japanese American culture. The Adlerian counselor begins the initial session with Yuri and Jonathon by disclosing his familiarity (and lack of knowledge) with the Japanese culture since he is a Caucasian American. He shares that he visited Japan 4 years ago and how that experience really sparked his interest in the Japanese culture and people. The counselor also acknowledges his limited understanding of Japanese traditions and culture and asks if Yuri and Jonathon could please enlighten him on certain facts about the culture and how Japanese people interact that he may not know. By honoring the cultural differences, the counselor has already paved the way for a relationship based on mutual respect and understanding. The counselor then invites Yuri and Jonathon to share their stories and worldviews. This allows the counselor to get a sense of what the subjective reality is for Yuri and Jonathon and to pay particular attention to particular themes that may arise for each of them.

Jonathon is the more talkative of the couple since Yuri is deferent to her husband and he speaks fluent English. He appears to be quite comfortable with the counseling process and openly shares his perspective of their situation. It is clear that Jonathon does not understand why Yuri is having such a difficult time adapting to life in America since he was able to integrate into the Japanese culture when he lived in Japan. The more Jonathon talks about Yuri's difficulty, the more Yuri withdraws.

Because of her traditional Japanese upbringing and the shame that is attached to disclosing family matters, Yuri already is feeling very embarrassed, timid, and inferior. The Adlerian counselor acknowledges how uncomfortable this must be for Yuri and addresses her courage to come to counseling. Although Yuri was very intimidated, she appears more relaxed as the counselor encourages her. She remains extremely polite and respectful to the counselor and, through her broken English and thick Japanese accent, she describes some of the physical complaints that she has experienced since migrating to America. It is very apparent that Yuri views the counselor as an expert, hoping that he could "fix" everything or give them specific advice to solve their problems.

Since Adlerians view the counseling relationship as one that is equally based on mutual cooperation and respect, the counselor used this opportunity to encourage Yuri and to acknowledge what a big step she had made to initiate counseling. This encouragement enables Yuri to feel more equal and worthy of her opinions. (The counselor also makes a mental note to revisit and address Yuri's feelings of inferiority after they had established a solid and trusting relationship.) Acknowledging that this couple is looking for an expert who can "fix" their situation, the Adlerian counselor assumes a more directive role, by suggesting that the couple complete the lifestyle assessment. The counselor takes a psychoeducational role by explaining that the assessment will help to examine the couple's lifestyles, their family dynamics, and experience from their childhood and families of origin, and how these tools and assessments can help the couple to establish some mutual goals with the counselor.

The second phase of counseling (the assessment phase) lasts for several sessions, and while continuing to build on the therapeutic relationship, the counselor conducts a lifestyle assessment with the couple. This lifestyle assessment evaluates how Yuri and Jonathon each define themselves within the current culture (American) while maintaining an understanding that they are each a product of their family histories and ancestries. This assessment proves to be a valuable resource because it gathers information about Yuri and Jonathon's marriage, their families of origin, their family constellations, their relationship to and with work, how they interact with others, their worldview, their support systems, their perspective roles as a man, a woman, and a husband and wife, and their feelings about themselves.

Because Yuri presented with depression and somatic symptoms, the counselor is also interested in assessing just how severe Yuri's depression is. He explores how she has coped with stressful situations in the past, as well as delving into her psychological and medical history. The counselor is particularly interested in what strengths Yuri has and what she has found that has helped her in the past. Because the counselor is aware of Yuri's traditional Japanese upbringing, he also explores certain Eastern holistic concepts of health and illness and tailors these concepts into the therapy.

As Yuri and Jonathon reveal personal details of their family constellations and early recollections, certain themes evolve that the therapist is quick to pick up on. Yuri reveals that she is a middle child from a family of six children. She is the fourth-born and the second oldest daughter. Yuri shares that she comes from a family that values males and is very traditional. Yuri shared that she was very shy as a child and was extremely close to her mother and older sister. Yuri found her place within the family by being extremely accommodating and by helping her mother to care for her younger siblings. Yuri also shared that she was extremely devout to her Buddhist religion and that it is through her strong religious beliefs that she finds her strength. Yuri also admits that she tends to be a pleaser and avoids confrontation at any costs. Her early recollections are indicative of her shy and pleasing nature. At age 6, she remembers the anger that her father displayed when she wanted to be like her brothers. She recalls the shame at displeasing her father and how she quickly learned that her place was in the house with her mother. At age 7, Yuri shares a memory of how she helped her mother make a special dish and how much fun she had working with her mother and her sisters. Her father was very pleased with how hard Yuri and her sisters had worked and said that she would make a good wife one day.

Jonathon, on the other hand, is an only child. His parents pampered him, and he was their world. He recalls how much his family wanted him to "fit in" with the other Americans in the town. Jonathon also shares some early recollections. At age 7, he was picked to play Joseph in the Christmas play at his Catholic elementary school. He remembers just how proud his parents were sitting in the audience and how proud he felt to have been picked for one of the starring roles in the play. His other recollection includes coming in second place in a baseball game and how hard it was to come in second when he knew that the team had played its best. Jonathon acknowledges that the strive for superiority played a significant factor in his life from an early age on. He was raised to always do his best and shares that he has little patience for people who do not seem to try their best. Jonathon points out that competition and doing your best is the "American way."

As the counselor gains an understanding of the dynamics and the private logic of Yuri and Jonathon, he helps them to understand their patterns of behavior and how it replays in their marriage. As Yuri and Jonathon become more aware and conscious of the impact of their behavior and some of their faulty beliefs and goals, they gain insight into how each of them are contributing to their current problems. Because the counselor has already established a trusting relationship with Yuri and Jonathon, he can make some hunches or "educated guesses" as to what he thinks might be the motivation or goals behind some of their behaviors.

Through the use of encouragement, interpretations, and education, the counselor is able to help Yuri and Jonathon to communicate more effectively as a couple and also to understand each other's past and how these learned behaviors are playing out in the marriage now. As Yuri and Jonathon become more aware of their behaviors and goals and the power that they each bring to the relationship, they can now start to assume a more active role in determining their future. The counselor continues to encourage each of them to recognize that they are the authors of their own lives and that both Yuri and Jonathon can choose to make different choices based on their newly gained insight and understanding. This is an active phase of therapy whereby both Yuri and Jonathon can transform their insights into new behaviors that will empower each of them and energize their relationship.

❧ Summary ❧

Adlerian counseling is a holistic approach based on encouragement and growth that respects Yuri and Jonathon as Japanese Americans while addressing their complex and varied counseling issues. As we can see from the presenting case and the breakdown of the various factors that affect Yuri and Jonathon, this is a complex case with many interlaced and interdependent issues. Adlerian therapy provides a broad and comprehensive foundation that can be tailored to honor all of the aspects that affect Yuri and Jonathon while respecting their individuality as well as their culture. The wide application of Adlerian psychotherapy, combined with its adaptability and holistic nature, allows for a comprehensive and integrative way to work with a couple such as Yuri and Jonathon from a multidimensional, holistic approach rather than using a surface application of either a family counselor, a career counselor, or a multicultural counselor.

❧ References ❧

Anderson, R. C., & Apostle, R. A. (1971). Occupational introversion–extroversion and size of hometown. *Vocational Guidance Quarterly, 20,* 138-140.
Berg, I. K., & Miller, S. D. (1992). Working with Asian American clients: One person at a time. *Families in Society: The Journal of Contemporary Human Service, 73,* 356-363.

Beutell, N. J., & Berman, U. W. (1999). Predictors of work–family conflict and sat-isfaction with family, job, career, and life. *Psychological Reports, 85,* 893–903.

Carlson, J. D., & Carlson, J. M. (2000). The application of Adlerian psychotherapy with Asian-American clients. *Journal of Individual Psychology, 56,* 214–225.

Carlson, J. D., & Slavich, S. (1997). *Techniques in Adlerian psychology.* Bristol, PA: Accelerated Development.

Corey, G. (2001). *Theory and practice of counseling and psychotherapy* (6th ed.). Pacific Grove, CA: Brooks-Cole/Wadsworth.

Cox, R. D. (1970). *Youth into maturity.* New York: Mental Health Materials Center.

Dreikurs, R., & Mosak, H. H. (1966). The tasks of life: I. Adler's three tasks. *The Individual Psychologist, 4,* 18–22.

Dreikurs, R., & Mosak, H. H. (1967). The tasks of life: II. The fourth task. *The Individual Psychologist, 4,* 51–55.

Forest, L. (1994). Career assessment for couples. *Journal of Employments Counseling, 31,* 168–187.

Goldenberg, H., & Goldenberg, I. (1998). *Counseling today's families* (3rd ed.). Pacific Grove, CA: Brooks/Cole.

Jones, F., & Fletcher, B. C. (1993). An empirical study of occupational stress trans-mission in working couples. *Human Relations, 46,* 881–904.

Kuo, W. H. (1984). Prevalence of depression among Asian Americans. *Journal of Nervous and Mental Disease, 172,* 449–457.

Lee, E. (1996). Asian-American families: An overview. In M. McGoldrick, J. Giordano, & J. K. Pearce (Eds.), *Ethnicity and family therapy* (2nd ed., pp. 227–248). New York: Guilford Press.

Leong, F. T. L. (1985). Career development of Asian Americans. *Journal of College Student Personnel, 26,* 539–546.

Levinson, D. J. (1986). A conception of adult development. *American Psychologist, 41,* 3–13.

Matsui, W. T. (1996). Japanese families. In M. McGoldrick, J. Giordano, & J. K. Pearce (Eds.), *Ethnicity and family therapy* (2nd ed., pp. 268–280). New York: Guilford Press.

McGoldrick, M., Giordano, J., & Pierce, J. K. (Eds.). (1996). *Ethnicity and family therapy* (2nd ed.). New York: Guilford Press.

Pedersen, P. (1990). The multicultural perspective as a fourth force in counsel-ing. *Journal of Mental Health Counseling, 12,* 93–95.

Sandhu, D. S. (1997). Psychocultural profiles of Asian and Pacific Islander Americans: Implications for counseling and psychotherapy. *Journal of Multicultural Counseling and Development, 25,* 7–23.

Seligman, L. (1994). *Developmental career counseling and assessment* (2nd ed.). Thousand Oaks, CA: Sage.

Sewell, W. H., & Orenstein, A. M. (1965). Community of residence and occupa-tional choice. *American Journal of Sociology, 70,* 551–563.

Sue, D. W. (1990). Culture specific strategies in counseling: A conceptual frame-work. *Professional Psychology: Research and Practice, 21,* 424–433.

Sue, S., & Sue, D. W. (1990). *Counseling the culturally different: Theory and practice* (3rd ed.). New York: Wiley.

Tanaka, M. J. (1979). *Taijun kyfusho: Diagnostic and cultural issues in Japanese psychiatry.* Washington, DC: American Psychiatric Association.

Uba, L. (1994). *Asian Americans: Personality patterns, identity, and mental health.* New York: Guilford Press.

Watts, R. E. (1999). The vision of Adler: An introduction. In R. E. Watts & J. Carlson (Eds.), *Interventions and strategies in counseling and psychotherapy* (pp. 1-14). Philadelphia, PA: Accelerated Development/Taylor & Francis Group.

Strategies for Counseling Family Three: The Robinson Family

Victoria Foster, Karen Eriksen, and Garrett McAuliffe

Yvonne Robinson is a 36-year-old African American woman who is a single parent of three boys: Michael, 12; Lloyd, 13; and James, 7. She has worked in minimum-wage jobs and has been on and off welfare. A year ago, Yvonne completed an associate's degree in office management and took her first job in this new career. Not long after obtaining this job, Yvonne's live-in boyfriend, Bob, who is James's father, moved out of the house. To bridge the income gap his departure created, Yvonne took a second job in a grocery store two evenings per week and all day Saturday and Sunday.

The children reacted very differently to Bob's departure. He has lived with Yvonne and her boys on and off for the past 5 years. The older children (who have a different father) seemed indifferent to his leaving, but James has started acting out in school. In fact, he has been suspended for angry temper tantrums, shouting, and cursing at his teachers. Yvonne has had to leave work many times to attend conferences about James's behavior.

Yvonne asked Bob, who is currently between construction jobs, to attend school conferences for her, but he has missed appointments that he promised to attend. Alternatively, Yvonne asked her sister, Marie, to attend these conferences for her, but the school is resistant to this substitution. Marie is physically disabled from an injury on her job and has the time to go to the school during the day. Yvonne explained to the school that her sister knows her children very well because Marie takes care of the boys after school along with her own three children. Yvonne appreciates Marie's after-school supervision because Michael and Lloyd tend to tease James and play tricks on him if they are unsupervised. In addition, Yvonne lived with Marie when Michael and Lloyd were very young. The boys know and treat Marie as a parent and, because of Yvonne's two jobs, Marie spends more time with them than Yvonne does. The school still refuses to let Marie stand in for Yvonne.

Yvonne knows something must be done about James's behavior, but her boss has already warned her that she should not miss anymore time from the job. Also, the school has recommended counseling, and Yvonne does not know how she is going to afford counseling, either in terms of time or finances. Yvonne is considering sending James to live with her sister, Ida, who is single, lives in a different state, and has no children. That way James will be away from his brothers who tease him, he will not have to worry about his father disappointing him because his father will be too far away to visit, and, if he is away from all of this turmoil, he probably will not need counseling. Her sister is willing to take James. What Yvonne is most afraid of is losing her job and going back on welfare. Her mother worked hard— often at two jobs to raise her three children—and although they lived in low-income housing, they were never on welfare. The work ethic is strong in her family, and Yvonne is the only member of the family who has been on welfare. She does not want to have to do that again.

❧ Understanding the Client's Worldview ❦

We use four models of therapy to begin our understanding of the client's worldview: The out-of-the-box model (this volume), a cultural group membership model (McAuliffe, 2001), a contextual–developmental model (McAuliffe & Eriksen, 1999), and feminist models of family therapy (Worell & Remer, 1992). These frameworks prompt us as counselors to examine the lenses through which we understand both the client's and our own worldview.

The out-of-the-box model has been sufficiently explained in chapter 2. The cultural group membership model expands the out-of-the-box model somewhat and is represented by the acronym GARREACS, which stands for Gender, Age, Race, Religion, Ethnicity, Ability, Class, and Sexual orientation. The contextual–developmental model is represented by the acronym CPSS, which stands for Context, Phase, Stage, and Style. The CPSS model combines four pathology-free worldviews into a reminder to counselors of how they might assess and counsel from a holistic and developmental perspective. A feminist family counseling perspective provides a dynamic framework for addressing the interactions among race, gender, and class and their relationship to power, family structure, and family processes. The key to this perspective is balancing the needs both within the family system and between the family and the related subsystems within which it resides.

On the basis of these models, we begin by forming hypotheses about how the client's current family and career experiences might be influenced by power relationships, by all of the cultural components (which are the same as the Context component of the CPSS model), and by the Phase and Stage components of the CPSS model.

Yvonne's (and Her Sons') Experience of Family

We assume that Yvonne is experiencing a variety of emotions related to her conflicting family roles. First of all, she is a *mother*. In that role, she has responsibility for her children's upbringing and well-being. Many African American parents, especially mothers, feel a sense of anxiety and helplessness about their ability to protect their male children (Boyd-Franklin & Bry, 2000). Moreover, single mothers tend to be considered inadequate to the tasks of raising male children and may internalize this societal perspective (Silverstein & Rashbaum, 1994).

We assume that up to this point, Yvonne shared her parenting responsibilities with Bob to some degree, responsibilities that included loving and disciplining the children as well as providing for their financial, safety, and physiological needs. However, what is not clear is the degree to which Bob shared in those responsibilities. We might be informed by research that indicates that even mothers who work outside the home continue to perform two thirds of the household and child-care responsibilities (Bromet, Dew, & Parkinson, 1990; Facione, 1994; Frone, Russell, & Cooper, 1991; Parker, 1997; Theorell, 1991). We might also be informed by looking at what we know of Bob's patterns of family interaction. For instance, after Bob moved out, he did not follow through on attending school conferences, and he is evidently not providing adequately for the family's financial needs. So if we assume that he remains true to such patterns, we might also assume that Yvonne is familiar with shouldering the lion's share of the household and parenting responsibilities. In this case, she may not be experiencing emotional distress about the change in her level of responsibility for the children vis-à-vis Bob's leaving. However, the fact that she must take on a second job because of the lack of his financial contributions brings her greater stress in figuring out how to manage the conflict between providing for the children's financial and physiological needs and their love and discipline needs. Any assessment must include an understanding of Yvonne's own needs and capabilities as the head of a single-parent family and an awareness of the social and economic issues at work in this situation.

Yvonne has also been a *life partner* and has lost this partnership, at least in its live-in capacity. It is difficult to know what Yvonne may be feeling about this loss, as it is at least partly dependent on the nature of her relationship with Bob before he left and the nature of the relationship once they are separated. Bob has clearly left before, and she is probably quite aware about what she can expect from the relationship following his departure. However, we do know that any major change in family relationships, such as this one, adds stress (Holmes & Rahe, 1967) and that Yvonne will need to address feelings of loss and grief related to change in the status of her relationship. In addition, to inform our awareness of the emotional impact of his leaving, we may want to discover the answers to the following questions: What was the quality of Bob and Yvonne's relationship during the last 5 years? How much did she depend on him emotionally? How strong did she experience their emotional bond to be? Were they in frequent conflict, and does she find it a relief to have a break from him? Or were they together for convenience sake, and whether he lives there or not does not affect her much emotionally or change her daily behavior or parenting to a significant degree? What expectations does she have about love relationships on the basis of her family-of-origin experience, her past love relationship experiences, and messages from her ethnic and racial cultural groups? What sort of relationship will Bob and Yvonne maintain now that they are separated? Does she expect him to return as he had in the past? If so, how long does she expect him to be away? Will they remain in communication while he is away? Does she anticipate that he will contribute anything financially, based on her previous experiences of his leaving? The answers to such questions will give us a clearer idea about Yvonne's experience of having her life partner move out.

Yvonne is also a member of an *extended family*, and her relationships with her extended family will clearly affect and be affected by both her mothering role and the quality of her dependence on her life partner. Her sister, Marie, has played a very important role in coparenting her children, taking care of the boys after school. Yvonne, through Marie's role in her children's lives, has succeeded in both assuring that she can work outside of the home and that her children are well taken care of. If Yvonne has just finished an associate's degree, we can also assume that she has relied on others to take care of her children while she attended school and completed schoolwork. It would also be important to assess the relationship her other sister, Ida, has with James during the decision-making process, because a counselor would need to be clear that Ida will be able to help him adjust to the losses inherent in having less contact with his mother and father. However, in this family, as in many African American families, family members help out. Nuclear families do not raise children alone. Therefore, Yvonne is not changing any family patterns in requesting Marie's further help in school conferences or Ida's help in taking James into her home. She is likely shocked that the school system will not accept her perspective that Marie would be an adequate and effective stand-in at school conferences. She is less likely than parents of the dominant culture, however, to feel guilt about asking her family to help out or to feel as though she has somehow failed as a parent because of the need to ask for such help.

Yvonne's *sons' perspectives* also need to be considered. James's misbehavior demonstrates a rather expectable reaction to major shifts in the family structure. Whether he feels most badly about his mother's absence, his father's leaving, or being the only sibling who cares about his father's leaving (being the odd one out), the current levels of support that he receives in his family are not enough for him. He may also be the one "selected" to be the symptom bearer for the family by nature of his being Bob's son. That is, he will not be the only one experiencing the family losses even though he is the only one "acting out" those losses. Counselors will need to attend to the other sons' experiences of the family shifts, despite their apparent absence of symptoms. Michael and Lloyd's symptoms may not be as dramatic or visible, or they may have other resources that James does not have. At age 7, James would be developmentally unable to verbally request what he needs from the adults in his life, and therefore he would act out his unmet needs. Michael and Lloyd may be more able to express their needs, and in doing so, may be more appropriately able to grieve their losses.

Other cultural factors intersect with Yvonne's family roles. For instance, individuals from *lower socioeconomic classes* may have a less internalized sense of control over life circumstances, which can lead to frustration, anger, and possibly learned helplessness (Boyd-Franklin & Bry, 2000). For Yvonne, this may also mean that she does not expect to have the control over her life that people from the dominant culture might expect to have. She may "give in" to circumstances, not expecting that she will have a say or that there is anything she can do about them. Furthermore, African American families may exhibit "healthy cultural suspicion" as a result of multigenerational experiences with racism and discrimination (Boyd-Franklin & Bry, 2000). Thus, Yvonne and her family may resist the intrusion of outside interventions in what is considered to be private family business.

In addition, those working at *low-wage jobs* that require little education realistically often have far fewer choices about work tasks, work schedules, and time off. Therefore, it is understandable that Yvonne's current family demands might threaten her employment. Furthermore, those at lower socioeconomic status (SES) levels are most likely to be concerned with meeting the lower levels of Maslow's hierarchy of needs (Maslow, 1987) and may thus be reluctant to pursue the more esoteric and longer term approaches to therapy: that is, those involving discovering one's self, one's feelings, and one's thoughts and those uncovering unresolved childhood conflicts, with the thought that insight will eventually lead to life change.

The Family–School Interface

School systems operating from the bias of the dominant culture expect and work hard to get parents involved in partnering with them for the benefit of their children's education. Furthermore, when children begin having trouble at school, school personnel expect parents to take action to "fix the problem." These expectations are not unreasonable unless schools fail to expand their definitions of "parent" beyond the nuclear family, fail to find ways to work with single-parent families beyond expecting them to behave as dual-parent families, and fail to interact with parents at any time but regular school hours. Only the dominant culture places such great pressures on nuclear families. Other cultures expand such expectations to the village of church, extended family, neighborhoods, and other adults trusted by the family. Only parents in higher SES brackets tend to have the freedom to miss work for consults with counselors and teachers during school hours. So although many of us might say "of course" to the school's requirements that Yvonne participate in conferences during school hours for the purposes of correcting her son's behavior, a more enlightened approach might understand the societal values reflected in this perspective and might further advocate for a shift in those values to values more conducive to Yvonne's contexts.

The Family–Community Interface

The case indicates nothing about Yvonne's involvement in a church community, but since religion and spirituality play such important roles in African American culture, it would be important to assess her involvement and the degree to which she might draw strength and support from that involvement. A counselor in a church or elders and ministers in her church might be able to provide counseling and "case management" at a price she can afford. African American churches are known for providing practical types of support. They might be able to provide financial assistance or to prevail on Bob to provide child or spousal support. In terms of comfort needs, they would certainly offer prayer and spiritual assistance. On the basis of Maslow's (1987) hierarchy of needs, the sort of practical help and connections to resources that a church might provide may be much more useful to Yvonne than formal counseling.

Career Context

For many lower-middle-class and working-class people, the very notion of "career" as a self-chosen path is foreign. "Work" is what you do to survive, and "a job" is where you work. Thus, we must first understand the place of work and career in Yvonne's world. To do so, two rubrics seem helpful: "internal" and "external" factors.

Internal Factors and Career

Aspirations. The counselor might first explore Yvonne's career aspirations, if they are articulable at this time at all. However, before imposing a middle-class bias that views "self-fulfillment through career," the counselor needs to ask Yvonne about her beliefs and ideas about working. Does she share the view common to working-class people that work is a necessary drudgery, an unfortunate accompaniment to the more important life centers of family, relationships, and community? Or does Yvonne treat work as a source of identity that gives profound meaning to everyday life? We suspect that she might be torn between these two notions and that her notion of career might be emerging, as a result of her new socialization through the community college experience.

The "Match". Another, and related, internal factor is that of the congruence, or "match," between who Yvonne is and what work she is doing. How did she choose office administration? There is often an arbitrary, class-related dimension in many first-generation college students' career choices, one characterized by a drive to "make good money in a field in which I can find a job easily in this local area." Inherent career interest and satisfaction are secondary. And yet the normative drumbeat of fulfillment through work has been heard in recent years and is one that is repeated in the professional literature and the popular media alike. It would be important to know how well matched Yvonne is to her occupation. Does she have the clerical and detail inclinations that office work requires for success and for satisfaction? In Holland's (1985) code terms, is she sufficiently oriented toward a "conventional" environment? Or did she choose the field in a less intentional fashion, perhaps now finding herself dreading the hours in the office? To help Yvonne understand her feelings about her work at this time, a counselor's task would be to raise these questions, ever so gently, with probes such as, "How are you doing at work?" "At what do you do best?" and "What do you like about the work?" Godfredson's (1996) person-environment match instrument might reveal a disparity between who Yvonne is and the work environment that she is in. Answers to such assessments could be logged away for future reference, when financial pressures are less the driving force for choosing a job. We might suspect at this point, however, that Yvonne is glad to have a job and that questions of job satisfaction are minor compared with the other issues in her life.

Attitude Toward Family Role Versus Career Role. At 36, with children ranging from ages 7 to 13, Yvonne has been parenting for a while. The salience of her mothering role may be reduced and the salience of her career role may be increasing as the children grow older. Her timing challenges the dominant middle-class discourse regarding traditional career development trajectories; in that narrative, Yvonne would be finished with school and would have begun establishing her career during her 20s, so that she would feel more stable, careerwise, during her 30s. This dominant narrative of a "right order" for the life script is confounded by research indicating that increasing numbers of women begin their formal education after childbearing.

Whatever the ages that women choose career or family as a focus, their struggle to manage both work and family responsibilities and the associated physical and psychological distress have been well documented in the literature (Bromet et al., 1990; Facione, 1994; Frone et al., 1991; Theorell, 1991). Housework and caring for the family remains socially constructed as women's work, despite women's acquisition of outside employment (Parker, 1997). Risk factors associated with this role combination include fatigue, depression, and stress (Derry & Gallant, 1993; Wheatley, 1991). Christian and Wilson (1985) found that women's worries as they enter or reenter the labor force or higher education involve concern over managing efficiently at home and performing successfully in school or on the job while coping effectively with a changing self-image. These women bring these concerns and risks with them into the vocational guidance arena. "Not only does the reentry woman need to make vocational choices that will enhance her self-esteem and autonomy; she needs to develop coping strategies that will enable her to function effectively in her multiple roles" (Christian & Wilson, 1985, p. 497).

Effective models of career counseling for reentry dual-career women must consider not only appropriate vocational choice but also the important issues of women's self-image and their construction of personal and interpersonal meaning within multiple roles. Women's career development occurs within a larger context of sex role socialization and institutionalized sexism that influence behavior and choices. Sex role socialization varies across racial, ethnic, and socioeconomic groups, however, and therefore women will experience the home–career conflict with various degrees of intensity (Worell & Remer, 1992). The absence of a supportive social climate for a humane integration of family and work responsibilities makes a decision to reenter the workforce especially problematic for many women (Morgan & Foster, 1999).

For these reasons, Yvonne's counselor might actively inquire as to how much ambivalence and distress accompanies time away from her children. We do know that Yvonne cannot seem to find a balance, as demonstrated by the conflict between work hours and children's needs. It is important that we assess the psychological (and physical) toll that this conflict brings for her, as well as the toll taken by working at least 66 hours per week. The counselor might ask, "What does Yvonne do for herself?" and "How does she take care of herself?"

External Factors and Career

Family Support. Yvonne seems to have strong family support from her siblings. That connectedness might hold her both emotionally and functionally. It would be important for the counselor to help Yvonne to maximize such support, especially under such trying circumstances as a 66-hour workweek, having three almost-adolescent boys, and financial hardship. The counselor can help Yvonne to maintain networks so that she has child care and some comfort in knowing that her children are being attended to. That might allow her to dedicate herself to her work more fully.

Professional Training. Yvonne has a solid credential that she might use in many settings. Thus job security should not be a major concern. The counselor can help Yvonne to recognize the power of her training, and perhaps, in the long run, assist her in advancing in her career. Without such encouragement and information, Yvonne might remain in minimum-wage jobs with few benefits, and that in turn might result in her family living below the poverty level or returning to welfare.

Work Hours. Yvonne is working during most of her waking hours. Although this may seem to be the only choice at this time, the counselor needs to assist her to find other future choices. In addition, the counselor may help her to assess her current emotional and physical status by asking questions such as: How can she maintain relationships in her life? How does she get enough rest? What psychic toll does this much work take? What are her concerns about having a life partner? What does she do to take care of herself?

Oppression and Bias Issues. Yvonne is an inheritor of an American legacy of racism and exclusion of "others" (i.e., those who are not White males) from positions of influence. In light of that legacy, the counselor may need to help Yvonne assess the type of organization she works for (e.g., using Jackson's model of stages of multiculturalism in organizations; see Jackson & Holvino, 1993). Are there exclusionary social networks at work, with the accompanying lack of access to gossip and information? If that is the case, does it add to her stress and sense of life frustration? Or does Yvonne sense some control in her workplace? A sense of control and being appreciated have been shown to be the highest sources of work satisfaction. Knowing the type of organization she works for may help Yvonne assess her workplace choices, which may in turn help her to gain greater control in her workplace.

Financial Stresses and Needs. Yvonne is under great financial strain; that fact frequently colors all other issues. She has three children and probably a relatively low wage. The counselor might serve as an advocate for Yvonne's getting substantial financial support from the fathers of her children.

Yvonne's Children's Careers

Guidance, Course Selection, and Tracking. Yvonne's children's "careers" also weigh in as factors in systems-oriented counseling. Lloyd is on the verge of high school and thus needing guidance about course, career, and future options. His school counselor could meet with him to make recommendations and to support his decision making. However, because of historical and systemic racial and economic bias, the family counselor may need to advocate to ensure that he receives the services to which he is entitled.

Male Models and Mentoring. All three of Yvonne's children could use male models of career and community success at this time, if their fathers are not present to them. Such men may be available through school, religious groups, or sports settings. School counselors, coaches, and religious leaders may need to be involved in helping the boys to develop such relationships.

Enrichment and Supplemental Learning Opportunities. Yvonne is not likely to have access to the middle-class enrichment activities that supplement children's schooling—the afternoon tutoring, the music lessons, the summer enrichment camps. Class- and race-related barriers will have to be overcome, as the peer groups in these settings are often predominantly White and middle class. Financial aid and scholarships will have to be sought. Car pooling will have to be arranged. Knowing the networks and making the arrangements for such experiences can be daunting to working-class individuals. Thus they often are shut out of these networks. Her family counselor and the school counselor can lead the family to these opportunities and help them gain access.

Priorities and Lifestyle Focal Point

At this point, it is clear that Yvonne's priority is to ensure that her children's needs are adequately met. Unfortunately, as often happens in families with one parent who works in low-paying jobs, the means to meet the children's financial needs conflicts with what is needed to meet their emotional, relational, and school needs. Counseling, therefore, needs to assist Yvonne in discovering ways to meet these conflicting needs, by developing individual and family strengths and awareness or by augmenting the family resources with external resources.

꙳ Impact of Counselor Variables ꙳

Counselors of many different cultures might work with Yvonne and her family, as family counselors, as career counselors, or as school or church-based counselors. And ethical work would demand that each of these counselors, so as not to impose their own biases, examine the lenses through which they view Yvonne and her family, the counseling process, the definition of the problem, and possible solutions to be considered. However, because we (the chapter authors) are White, European American, middle-class professionals, we examine the intersection between counselors from the dominant culture and Yvonne and her family's needs. The assumption here is that the "control" over the counselor's values or over imposing such on the client generates from staying aware of one's own values and experiences, becoming aware of any client values and experiences that might differ, keeping both in the forefront of one's mind, hypothesizing about the impact of both on the counseling relationship, countering any unjustified natural inclinations emanating from those values and experiences, and dialoguing with Yvonne about both values and tendencies. We found that the values and experiences that might color our work with Yvonne were related to our European heritage, our perceptions of what is a "normal" family life, the current salience of our gender roles in our own families, our middle-class experiences and values, our constructive developmental stages, and the perspective of traditional counseling practice.

European Heritage

From most European American perspectives, one pulls oneself up by one's own bootstraps and can have control over one's life if one only works hard enough. Such a perspective is not reflective of many other cultural groups, particularly those that have been historically oppressed. As counselors, we would need to work hard to understand that rationally coming up with a plan to handle a situation does not necessarily guarantee a favorable result and that efficiency is not always a value for those we work with.

Furthermore, we have valued (and had the luxury of valuing) career choices that give us pleasure and fulfillment. We suspect the extreme work ethic as an imbalanced, joyless dictate and instead attempt to find joy in work, try to integrate play and work, and honor our body's rhythms in work. We value spontaneity and socializing as central life expressions and consider work as equal, or, ultimately, as secondary to those. These perspectives on work are certainly not widespread and may not be reflective of Yvonne's ideas about the relationship between her work life and her "other" life.

Therefore, with Yvonne, we would need to assess her values related to work and her sense of control over her work life. We would need to stay aware that she might not believe that she can find a workable answer and follow through on it, and that this belief might be quite rational considering life experiences of personal or racial discrimination. We will have to listen closely to the values expressed in how she spends her time, considering values other than efficient hard work, considering how such values might be used to solve the problems she is experiencing, and helping her to consider the benefits and limitations of various value choices.

"Normal" Family Life

Even those of us who have chosen nontraditional families still have ambivalent feelings related to valuing a nuclear family with a husband and wife and 2.2 children. Despite experiencing divorce, including non-nuclear family members in our homes at times, experiencing varieties of means of conceiving a child, and not always choosing legal marriage as the guideline for living with a life partner and children, we struggle to let go again and again of a culturally defined ideal that sees the nuclear, intact family as optimal. Although we have consciously worked at expanding those definitions to include newfound beliefs about the advantages of building a village and an extended family and friend system, and although we have opened our eyes to family systems and configurations in diverse cultures and situations, respecting the benefits of these systems over our limited family-of-origin experiences, we are still in process. We find that the pressures of the dominant system keep us alternating between trying to realize the dominant value and developing dynamic rather than static notions of culture in which no single family configuration is considered ideal. We imagine that these internal processes might limit us in considering all of the possibilities available to Yvonne and her family. For instance, for Yvonne's family, Ida might be the ideal parent for James at this time. We would thus need to counter-act any urge to keep the nuclear family together at all costs.

Related to our conceptions about nuclear families are our (Victoria's and Karen's) perceptions of motherhood. Our relationships with our children are grounded in our own life histories and circumstances and reflected in our respective family systems. It is from our constructions of motherhood and family that decisions about our children's health, education, and social development emerge. We would have to work hard at not imposing values on Yvonne. We would need to discover how, within the range of her choices and possibilities, she wanted to be a mother to her children.

A related issue would be our own need for the emotional support of a significant other, and the correlating grief inherent in conceiving of our own life partners leaving us. The variables of race, gender, and ethnicity affect the construction of family roles, expectations, and definitions of normalcy. We would need to understand Yvonne's perspective on this. Perhaps she would not expect a life partner to really stay for life. Perhaps her history with Bob would not lead her to feel devastated, as she knows he always comes back, or she respects his occasional need to wander, or she still has a relationship with him even when he is not living with her. Her self-reliance may be particularly strong; she may prefer her independence. Assessing and respecting Yvonne's particular perspectives on love relationships and the role she wants such relationships to play in her life would be part of understanding the impact of Bob's leaving.

Gender Roles

European American counselors spend a good deal of time helping women to become strong, able to take care of themselves, and able to rectify or leave bad relationships with men. However, it is difficult to maintain such a "self-righteously" strong position after having one's own child. The cultural imperatives experienced by both the male and female life partners are strong enough and salient enough that any expectations of equity in household work and parenting usually turn into myths.

From the male perspective, the cultural pressure to be the ultimate breadwinner and the sometimes missing domestic inclination may make it difficult to attend to important family needs. Our male author (Garrett) finds that career hangs so heavily on his sense of identity and "being-in-the-world" that he has to make conscious efforts to counter inclinations and socialization (and rewards!) so that he "makes time" for family instead of engaging in more autonomous activities. Despite beliefs in the importance of family, he does not experience the excruciating and conflict-generating pull toward child rearing that many women (not all!) do. We are all still in process around these issues as well.

We would have to work hard to own our own anger at the injustice Yvonne is experiencing and to temper our judgments about her life choices with respect for the cultural systems that influence all people. Our own perspectives could inform the counseling process, but not to the neglect of allowing her perspectives to inform the dialogue as well.

Middle-Class Background

Our middle-class backgrounds might limit us in other ways as well. They would define our understandings of family, finances, and career possibilities in ways that Yvonne might not define her own. Furthermore, we have not had experiences with the social service systems that someone struggling with welfare issues might have had. Our lack of experience might lead us to believe that certain resources ought to be available to Yvonne and her family and to urge Yvonne to make use of such resources when they are not really available. For instance, in many places, community services boards may be mandated to provide counseling services for people like Yvonne but may have 6- to 12-month waiting lists for receiving such services. We would need to keep in mind that someone who had lived a life of poverty, had struggled to get off welfare, and had lived among others who had struggled financially would likely be far more able to inform us about the intricacies of accessing other sorts of resources and negotiating social systems. We would thus need to balance our efforts at empowering Yvonne with what might become very real needs to advocate for her.

Constructive Developmental Stage

According to Kegan (1994), the ways in which people construct or know reality both constrain and limit their knowing and behaving. At certain constructive developmental stages, they may become more capable of conceptualizing the need for systems change and of balancing the needs of different, intersecting systems. Initially, as counselors, we may find ourselves wanting to advocate for those who might need it "against" the system that is "doing them wrong." This perspective is rather shortsighted because, while systemic oppressions do exist and we need to both be aware of them and counter the oppressions, individuals such as Yvonne find their own ways to develop competencies and creative solutions that enable them to thrive. So, we would need to constrain ourselves from advocacy long enough to find ways to recognize power differentials in which Yvonne might benefit from advocacy and also to pursue more permanent systems change by building on Yvonne's evident strengths. The specific purpose would be to assist her family and cultural systems to communicate effectively with her school and work systems, hopefully with the end goal of better understandings being reached, long-held but unhelpful procedures being shifted, and all involved in the discussions growing in positive directions.

Traditional Counseling Approaches

Traditional models of 50-minute hour, in-the-office, talk therapy have become somewhat outdated as a result of mounting evidence that 80% of adults in the United States with mental health problems are not receiving adequate help (Lewis, Lewis, Daniels, & D'Andrea, 1998). When the

Substance Abuse Mental Health Services Association held congresses of mental health providers from all disciplines, the following reasons were cited for the current failure of the mental health care delivery system (Wohlford, Myers, & Callan, 1993):

1. Training students in traditional long-term models of counseling fails to prepare them for counseling in the public sector.
2. In particular, they are not prepared to deal with such vulnerable populations as the elderly, children, the chronically mentally ill, substance abusers and the dually diagnosed, and the poor and homeless.
3. They are not trained to access and build connections between varieties of human service institutions, and thus fail to help multi-need clients receive a coordinated system of care.
4. They are not equipped to assess and coordinate systems of care, and so services are often fragmented.
5. They are not well trained in models of therapy that are more help-ful for those functioning at lower developmental levels.

When multicultural counselors (e.g., Sue & Sue, 1990) write about the current system's failure, they indicate that graduates are not well prepared to serve those from the nondominant culture. They indicate that traditional diagnostic and treatment models fit Eurocentric culture better than they do many other cultures. Thus, the traditional models continue the oppressions that many from nondominant cultures experience. Furthermore, if systems are dysfunctional or perpetuating oppressions, viewing clients within these systems as disordered does not address the problem. Multicultural counselors suggest that to be effective with those from other cultures, counselors need to be part of the communities the prospective clients inhabit. Counselors may need to provide services in community organizations, such as churches or community centers, where prospective clients gather. Counselors need to work with, rather than against, the indigenous healers in these other cultures. Counselors may need to adopt more directive approaches and more fully use psychoeducational tools. And counselors may need to learn to create systems change, rather than focusing only on individuals.

Herein lies the problem: Those in a counseling practice may find themselves structured around the 50-minute billable hour. If they are to make a living that depends on insurance payments, they are limited as to how much time they can spend on such activities as systems change, advocacy for clients, pro bono work, coordination of services, psycho-educational approaches in at-risk situations, presence in communities to take their "pulse," so to speak, and meetings with community members.

Only counseling and therapy are reimbursed by the insurance companies; these other activities are not.

If we as counselors are truly committed to serving a more diverse group of people, then we need to shift away from a dependency on insurance payments as a sole means of income and perhaps be willing to make less of a living. For instance, we might work with others to develop a grant-funding base. However, as most counselors traditionally practice, meeting Yvonne and other diverse groups' needs means that counselors would be faced with a daily decision-making struggle between offering the poor and people with multiple needs the services they need and realizing that when doing so, counselors would be spending time away from the services that support their staying in practice.

Intersections Between Client's and Counselor's Contexts

In addition to considering Yvonne's perspectives based on the many contexts within which she operates and the counselor's perspectives based on his or her contexts, we should also consider the intersection between Yvonne's contexts and those of the counselor. That is, what might be Yvonne's likely reactions to a counselor who does not share her contexts? For example, when considering any of us (the chapter authors) as counselors, what might Yvonne's reactions be to receiving counseling from a White, middle-aged, middle-class counselor who has never been on welfare, always had a salaried professional job, and has not used extended family to a great degree in support of raising children? Might she feel there was no way for the counselor to understand her experience and therefore to help her? Might she feel comfort in her historical role of receiving help from someone from the dominant culture but find herself back in an unempowered role as a result? Would she feel comfortable in asking for a different sort of help if the help offered was not perceived as useful to her? Would she be able to overcome historical experiences of oppression to truly work collaboratively with the counselor to make her situation better? It is clear that the interactions between the counselor's and client's perspectives critically impact the counseling relationship and need to be considered when designing interventions.

❧ Helpful Interventions ❧

We would choose a systems ecological counseling approach that is consistent with the out-of-the-box model and that integrates the various contexts into assessment and intervention. The systems ecological orientation promotes a wider worldview with the following assumptions: (a) Each person is an inseparable part of a small social system, (b) disturbance is a discordance in the system rather than a problem within the person, and (c) discordance is defined as a disparity between an individual's abilities and the demands or expectations of the environment—a failure of the match between the person and the systems (Fine & Carlson, 1992; Sontag, 1996). The systems ecological paradigm becomes a framework within which existing techniques—such as collaborative consultation, family counseling, behavioral interventions, and problem-solving strategies—facilitate a match between the person and the systems (home, school, community) in which they are developing (Conoley & Conoley, 1992).

Feminist Family Therapy

Within the systems ecological paradigm, we would choose a number of elements proposed by feminist family therapy (Worell & Remer, 1992). For instance, we would challenge the restrictions of dominant models of masculine and feminine socialization. Challenging such restrictions might illuminate the lines of power, privilege, racism, gender schemas, and limiting assumptions that could inhibit healthy sexual and interpersonal development within Yvonne's family (Fish, 1989; Worell & Remer, 1992).

From such challenges emerge counseling techniques for engaging the family and facilitating change. For instance, creating a therapeutic environment depends on framing the work as collaborative and cooperative and on demystifying the therapeutic process for the family (Kogan, 1996). From another feminist perspective, the therapist becomes more of a consultant than an expert and offers encouragement to enable all family members to value their own experiences and ways of making meaning (Parvin & Biaggio, 1991). A focus on reducing the power differential between clients and therapist may also serve as a model for family and social relationships (Pilais & Anderton, 1986). Counseling contracts may contribute to clearly articulating the conditions of therapy and the therapeutic goals toward which the counselor and family will work (Worell & Remer, 1992, p. 103). However, despite all attempts to reduce power differentials, the implicitly hierarchical nature of the therapeutic relationship itself cannot be ignored, and the therapeutic relationship should be continuously examined to prevent replicating the dominant culture's power arrangements (Kogan, 1996).

Feminist family therapists also recognize that their own beliefs and values are present in their relationship with the family. Openness about these beliefs and philosophies is ethically necessary and creates the possibility of dialogue within the family about topics that may have been ignored or suppressed. For instance, unnoticed or invisible social sanctions may have been inhibiting discussion and restraining meaning making about complex topics such as single parenting, gender, and race (Kogan, 1996).The counselor works to counter such sanctions by initiating dialogue about how such important factors may influence individual and family lives, as well as the counseling process.

Counseling Process From the Systemic Ecological Perspective

Counselors operating from a systems ecological perspective have a wide range of strategies available to them; all of them consider the person's context and strive to intervene systemically.Therefore, we recommend the following steps in beginning the counseling process.

Step 1: Initial Meeting. The counselor would meet with Yvonne at a place and time that allows the whole family to be present, hopefully even Bob, Marie, and Ida. During the initial meeting, the counselor would begin the assessment, keeping in mind all of the potential cultural influences described above on the family, the counselor, and the counseling relationship.

Step 2: Systemic and Competency Focus. During the initial sessions, the counselor would particularly assess the family's strengths, successes, and competencies. Once assessed, the counselor would recognize and acknowledge all of the competencies that became apparent. For instance, rather than challenging Yvonne on neglecting James's needs in order to work a second job, we might say to Yvonne, "You really feel your responsibility to your children so strongly that you would sacrifice yourself to work two jobs in order to provide for them." Or rather than focusing on how James is "messing up," we might say to James, "You are so concerned about your mom and about keeping your family together that you were willing to sacrifice your own schoolwork to draw enough attention to your family needs so that someone would do something." We might help Yvonne to affirm her qualities and achievements (e.g., earning an associate's degree while parenting young children and working outside the home). Furthermore, we might acknowledge how well matched she is with her work (if that is the case) and evoke declarations of her achievements (see Bolles, 2001).We might also positively reframe the family's struggles as natural to the transition that has been forced on them. That is, we might emphasize the major changes that the family has experienced over the last year and suggest that sometimes families need assistance in figuring out how to transition to a new place when new needs arise.

Also during initial sessions, the counselor would assess values, attitudes, skills, and interests related to work. The counselor would determine Yvonne's satisfaction with her job, in particular being open to any racial discrimination issues (e.g., social isolation at work, lack of access to gossip networks, subservience expected) that she is affected by or concerned about or that add more stress. The counselor would ask Yvonne about the messages she received about career in her family (and ethnic or religious groups).

Step 3: Involving Other Systems. To avoid placing blame on the family for the problem, and to begin coordinating the systems of care that might be a source of both the problem and the solution, we would want to start discussing the involvement of broader systems right from the beginning of counseling. Therefore, we would obtain releases of information—as Yvonne felt comfortable doing so—to converse with other family members, church leaders (assuming this is relevant for Yvonne's family), key people at Yvonne's work, and school counselors, teachers, and principals. Our initial aim in contacting these others would be to get a sense of their perspectives on the problem, their perspectives on solutions and resources, and their willingness to meet with Yvonne and her family to create solutions and coordinate care.

We would then meet for an extended session with Yvonne (and key members of the family) and whatever members of her community were willing to meet. We would define the problem, help different systems understand how they are intersecting with and influencing this family, identify key resources within the different systems, and brainstorm about possible solutions. We would then develop "contractual" arrangements about what roles each system would play in the solutions, deciding on target dates for accomplishing these roles and for meeting to evaluate progress.

Possible ideas the group might consider include the following:

- The church might provide financial and material resources temporarily so that Yvonne does not have to work a second job. The resources might be provided until Bob returns, if we discover that that may happen, or until the courts can mandate his payments. The church might also offer a "big sister/big brother" arrangement to the children to support them through a difficult time.
- Bob could provide child and perhaps spousal support for same reasons. If he will not attend, or cannot be prevailed upon, Yvonne might be assisted to pursue such support through the courts. If he is willing to attend, the counselor would further assess his ability and willingness to be involved in the solution, including whether he can or will commit to maintaining a relationship with Yvonne and the kids through this difficult time.
- The school representatives could arrange to meet for conferences at a time when Yvonne does not have to work so that her job is not at risk when she is needed for school conferences. The school might also agree to let Marie substitute for Yvonne at parent conferences after coming to understand the importance of Yvonne's extended family in raising her children.

- The school could work with Yvonne and her boys to create shifts in the learning environment toward a better fit with Yvonne's children. In particular, assistance could be provided for Yvonne and her sisters in connecting with school counselors; with advisors who would help with course selection, "tracking," and future goal setting for the older boy; and with those who would assess her children's interests and potentials.
- The school could arrange for an "Askable Adult/Mentor" program (see Eberling-Still, in press) to provide positive models of academic success and stability, as well as other adults to care about them. The school counselor could connect Yvonne and her boys to enrichment opportunities such as after-school tutoring or free summer enrichment camps (see Taylor, in press).
- The work representative could offer greater flexibility to Yvonne, allowing her to make up hours missed for school conferences or other child-care functions, perhaps allowing her to take work home at night.
- All could decide that James would stay with Ida for a period of time until Yvonne and Bob could stabilize the family and financial situation.
- Financial advising assistance could be arranged to help Yvonne explore options on how to maximize her resources. By helping her to budget, she might make it financially without the extra job. She might explore alternative living situation options, such as living with family members.

Step 4: Ongoing Efforts at Family Change. Counseling would continue with Yvonne and pertinent members of her family to support their efforts at following through with their part of the change plan. Assets and obstacles to meeting the plan would be assessed in an ongoing basis. For instance, through conversation and observation, the counselor would assess

- the degree of family engagement and disengagement;
- the family's communication skills, including love language and conflict resolution ability;
- Yvonne, Marie, and Ida's strength as parent figures, including their strength at disciplining and nurturing;
- individual and collaborative needs for grieving the losses and changes in the family;
- parent figures' abilities to advocate for themselves with the systems with which they interact;
- sibling subsystem of warmth, nurturing, strength, and support ability.

Concurrently with assessment, the counselor would share his or her observations in competency terms and link these observations to the problems as Yvonne and her family see them. Together, they would set goals to (a) enhance the processes that are working well within the family, with individuals, and in family interactions with various outside systems and (b) shift the unhelpful processes of individuals, between family members, in family interactions with various outside systems.

During ongoing sessions, the counselor would work within the session to help the family meet these goals and would work outside of the sessions as needed as the facilitator or advocate between the family and the other systems. As successes emerge toward solving the problem, the counselor would celebrate with the family.

◆ Summary ◆

Counseling professionals are well situated to bring career, family, and contextual perspectives into an integrated strategy for working with families like Yvonne's. Our heritage includes vocational work; licensure laws are requiring family counseling courses more frequently; and we often lead the mental health profession in including diverse perspectives in our lifestyles, our counseling, and our associations. Therefore, this chapter has brought career counseling and awareness of counselor and client contextual factors into family and systemic work that helps Yvonne and her community to balance her needs to provide financially for her family with her needs to care lovingly for her family.

This approach is offered as an attempt to begin the conversation about the intersections among family, career, and multiculturalism in counseling practice. Incorporating a feminist perspective into the out-of-the-box framework has the potential to transform the family culture and also provides a guideline for moving the client toward thinking more complexly about herself and her experiences within the multiple roles she must undertake. These experiences take place in the context of numerous internal and external influences associated with gender bias and sex role socialization. Gender oppression, heterosexual presumption, racism, and sex role stereotyping limit women and men in their ability to create and maintain healthy, intimate, and egalitarian relationships. Intrinsic in our approach is the facilitation of agency and self-empowerment, such that Yvonne will be able to challenge past, present, and anticipated barriers to family satisfaction and career success.

What is also notable is the personal growth, empowerment, and challenging of unanticipated barriers that we experienced while writing this chapter. Although we have for many years been passionately committed to challenging our students and supervisees to think about context, we were amazed at the shifts in our own thinking that were brought about by forcing ourselves to explicitly spell out contextual factors that might play into Yvonne's situation and into our own counseling perspectives. In particular, we found ourselves more committed to engaging the larger community in defining both problems and solutions and being more creative in thinking about nonstandard solutions. We were reminded once again of the impossibility of extricating career from most other counseling issues, a position that has long been taken by the counseling profession in its requirements that counselors take a (often dreaded) course in career counseling. Perhaps a writing exercise such as this one should be required of all of us as we begin our work with clients. Certainly we will require more explicit writing about such factors in our future work with supervisees.

As we leave Yvonne and her family, perhaps we ought to leave with this caveat: Only in ongoing work with this family can we come to know the answers to many of the questions posed in this chapter. As we engage in the recursive process of meeting, engaging, asking, listening, relating, and intervening over and over again, we will come to know the depths of Yvonne and her family, of ourselves as counselors of this family, of society's impact on the family, and of cultural influences on the counseling relationship. Although we have suggested hypotheses to consider, all should be tested out in the arena of "real life" before conclusions can be drawn. And even after drawing conclusions, we should be open to the changing, emerging, developing possibilities for all of the individuals and systems we encounter during "treatment" of this family.

∿ References ∾

Bolles, R. (2001). *What color is your parachute?* Berkeley, CA: Ten Speed Press.

Boyd-Franklin, N., & Bry, B. H. (2000). *Reaching out in family therapy: Home-based, school, and community interventions.* New York: Guilford Press.

Bromet, E. J., Dew, M. A., & Parkinson, D. K. (1990). Spillover between work and family: A study of blue-collar working wives. In J. Eckenrode & S. Gore (Eds.), *Stress between work and family* (pp. 133–151). New York: Plenum Press.

Christian, C., & Wilson, J. (1985). Reentry women and feminist therapy: A career counseling model. *Journal of College Student Personnel, 26,* 496–500.

Conoley, J. C., & Conoley, C. W. (1992). *School consultation practice and training* (2nd ed.). Boston: Allyn & Bacon.

Derry, P., & Gallant, S. (1993). Motherhood issues in the psychotherapy of employed mothers. *Psychiatric Annals, 23,* 432–437.

Eberling-Still, T. (in press). Models and mentors: Bringing askable adults into young people's lives. In G. McAuliffe (Ed.), *Working with troubled youth in schools: A guide for all school staff.* Westport, CT: Greenwood.

Facione, N. (1994). Role overload and health: The married mother in the waged labor force. *Health Care for Women International, 15,* 157–167.

Fine, J. J., & Carlson, C. (1992). *The handbook of family-school intervention: A systems perspective.* Boston: Allyn & Bacon.

Fish, L. S. (1989). Comparing structural, strategic, and feminist-informed family therapies: Two Delphi studies. *American Journal of Family Therapy, 17,* 303–314.

Frone, M. R., Russell, M., & Cooper, M. L. (1991). Relationship of work and family stressors to psychological distress: The independent moderating influence of social support, mastery, active coping, and self-focused attention [Special issue: Handbook on job stress]. *Journal of Social Behavior and Personality, 6,* 227–250.

Godfredson, G. (1996). *Using the Holland occupational-environmental classification in research and practice.* ERIC Document Reproduction Service No. ED 334408.

Holland, J. L. (1985). *Making vocational choices.* Englewood Cliffs, NJ: Prentice Hall.

Holmes, T. H., & Rahe, R. H. (1967). The Social Readjustment Rating Scale. *Journal of Psychosomatic Research, 11,* 213–218.

Jackson, B., & Holvino, E. (1993). Multicultural organization development. *Journal of College Student Development, 34,* 201–205.

Kegan, R. (1994). *In over our heads: The mental demands of modern life.* Cambridge, MA: Harvard University Press.

Kogan, S. (1996). Clinical praxis: Examining culture and power in family therapy. *Journal of Feminist Family Therapy, 8*(3), 25–44.

Lewis, J. A., Lewis, M. D., Daniels, J. A., & D'Andrea, M. J. (1998). *Community counseling: Empowerment strategies for a diverse society.* Pacific Grove, CA: Brooks/Cole.

Maslow, A. (1987). *Motivation and personality.* New York: Harper & Row.

McAuliffe, G. J. (2001). Identifying cultural group memberships: An introductory activity. In G. J. McAuliffe & K. P. Eriksen (Eds.), *Classroom strategies for constructivist and development counselor education* (pp. 87–93). Westport, CT: Bergin & Garvey.

McAuliffe, G. J., & Eriksen, K. P. (1999). Toward a constructivist and developmental identity for the counseling profession: The context-phase-stage-style model. *Journal of Counseling and Development, 77,* 267–280.

Morgan, B., & Foster, V. (1999). Vocational counseling for reentry dual career women: A cognitive developmental approach. *Journal of Career Development, 26,* 125–136.

Parker, L. (1997). Keeping power issues on the table in couples work. *Journal of Feminist Family Therapy, 9*(3), 1–24.

Parvin, R., & Biaggio, M. K. (1991). Paradoxes in the practice of family therapy. *Women & Therapy, 11*(2), 3–12.

Pilais, J., & Anderton, J. (1986). Feminism and family therapy: A possible meeting point. *Journal of Family Therapy, 8,* 99–114.

Silverstein, O., & Rashbaum, B. (1994). *The courage to raise good men.* New York: Viking Press.

Sontag, J. C. (1996). Toward a comprehensive theoretical framework for disability research: Bronfenbrenner revisited. *Journal of Special Education, 30,* 319–344.

Sue, D. W., & Sue, D. (1990). *Counseling the culturally different*. New York: Wiley.

Taylor, R. (in press). Go where they are: Reaching out to parents. In G. McAuliffe (Ed.), *Working with troubled youth in schools: A guide for all school staff*. Westport, CT: Greenwood.

Theorell, T. (1991). Psychosocial cardiovascular risks—on the double loads in women. *Psychotherapy and Psychosomatics, 55,* 81–89.

Wheatley, D. (1991). Stress in women. *Stress Medicine, 7,* 73–74.

Wohlford, P., Myers, H. F., & Callan, J. E. (Eds.). (1993). *Serving the seriously mentally ill: Public-academic linkages in services, research and training*. Washington, DC: American Psychological Association.

Worell, J., & Remer, P. (1992). *Feminist perspectives in therapy: An empowerment model for women*. West Sussex, England: Wiley.

Part IV

❦

New Directions

∾ Chapter 7 ∾

Research in Context

Lisa D. Hawley, Jane Goodman, and Mary Shaieb

As the earlier chapters of this book demonstrate, looking at work, family, and culture together provides greater explanatory power than looking at any one or two of these elements. Our aim in this chapter is to summarize the current status of the research, including the integration of the variables related to culture and family. Suggestions for areas for future investigation are also provided. Because of the complexity of the individual, it is difficult to say "this tool is for this client." The out-of-the-box model includes many variables well documented in the career field, such as values, abilities, gender, and ethnicity. Yet, the current status of career research lacks models and research that articulate or integrate the variables in the out-of-the-box model. The editors of this volume advocate the notion that counselors "have a professional responsibility to grow." Similarly, as researchers, we have a professional responsibility to grow in our research methods, ideologies, and frameworks.

Career transitions, choice, and stability are incorporated into the daily contextual issues of everyday life. The last few decades have included a flurry of research in the area of multicultural counseling that includes race, gender, socioeconomic status, disability, sexual orientation, religious issues, and the like. But, according to Lewis and Arnold (1998), multiculturalism is not simply the acquaintance with the customs of distant populations, tolerance of differences, and understanding cross-cultural communication. Multiculturalism is knowing and understanding that both the counselor and client are complex cultural beings.

Couple and family therapy continues to develop as a field, providing strong theoretical contributions and research regarding the workings of couples and families. The expansive field of couple and family counseling includes a history of research focusing on couples, parent–child interactions, family histories, and various family patterns and dynamics. Throughout this chapter, we take the position that an individual's career journey includes influences such as family involvement and values, ethnicity, educational environment, economic conditions, and personal values. Evans and Rotter (2000) addressed the complexity of integrating consideration of family and cultural influences as counselors expand their understanding and practice of career counseling.

Because the complexity of individuals and the layering of outside influences have an impact on the individual, the ability to understand, compare, and describe the intricacies of an individual's inner and outer experiences requires a broad range of research methods. Therefore, the researcher needs to think out of the box, integrating a variety of research methods, describing and comparing a number of variables, and using continual innovation in describing and understanding the complexity of the individual and the counseling process.

The research that is described tends to be defined within the respective fields of couple and family therapy, multicultural counseling, or career development. There is little research integrating the three components. Most often, the research consists of a discussion of career within the framework of an ethnic population, gender, or socioeconomic status, to describe a few, or an investigation of career within families or couples. It is difficult to find increased understanding and investigation of the integration of these variables in the current research. Yet, as individuals, we are able to think of early cultural messages and family influences that affected our own career decisions and narratives. The state of the economy, parental influences, expected standard of living, educational background, family background, critical national events, cultural messages regarding gender, race, religious upbringing, and socioeconomic status are all pieces that socially construct what we each think of career choice, stability, transition, and success. The current status of research provides a beginning to understanding the complex integration of the different influences creating individuals' views and experiences regarding their careers.

Families are an important socialization tool regarding work-related behavior (Brown, Brooks, & Associates, 1996). Families and culture are intertwined and are central components in the transmission of values of work and career. In this chapter, we identify the following: (a) research focusing on the role of families in career decisions, identity, and management; (b) research studying the influence of diversity and culture on career issues, focusing on choice, work experience, and social barriers; and (c) research that includes all three components of career, family, and multicultural studies in the field of counseling. Overall, our intention is to provide a summary of the current research describing the different variables included in the out-of-the-box model, as well as identifying research that looks at career as contextual. Limitations and strengths, as well as suggestions for the future direction of career counseling research, are also discussed.

≫ Family Life and Career Counseling ≪

Career choice, identity, and transitions are greatly influenced by family influence and roles. The present research on family and career tends to focus on several areas, including the role of the couple in career decisions, family–work conflict and balance, and family influence on young adults' decision making regarding career choice.

The relationship among couple influences, career choice, and the ability to maintain balance between family and career is a strong area of research. The basic themes in this research include family roles, balancing, and developmental cycles. Using scales that focus on marital adjustment, work–family conflict, and social support, Burley (1995) examined the variables that have an impact on work–family conflicts when both spouses are working. Burley found men and women demonstrated higher marital adjustment with partners if they experienced increased social support and time spent on household tasks. A common theme for today's couples and families is finding a balance of work, family, and personal satisfaction. Sinacore and Akcali (2000) studied the impact of the family environment on men's job satisfaction and self-esteem using the Four Component Self-Esteem Scale. They found that family environment had a limited impact on self-esteem. The research regarding couples also demonstrates that women stress familial issues as having an impact on work and career balances. Phillips-Miller, Campbell, and Morrison (2000) studied satisfaction, stress, and spousal support. A study of 242 married female veterinarians found that these women experienced significantly greater effect of marital/family stress on career and less perceived spousal support for career than did their male counterparts.

Another area of study is that of family influences and values on career decision making among young adults. Phillips, Christopher-Sisk, and Gravino (2001, p. 193) suggested that there are three overarching themes in looking at how young adults relate to their families in making career decisions: (a) the actions of others, in which the others offer advice, suggestions, orders, and so on; (b) recruitment of others, in which the decider seeks out input; and (c) pushing others away, in which others are actively excluded from the process. The family influence on career decision making ranges from subtle impacts such as family values to direct parental involvement. Amudson and Penner (1998) described a parent-involved career exploration method with students. Half of the students' responses were positive, whereas the rest of the students identified concerns including shyness and being embarrassed by parents' communication abilities. Some students found improvement in communication with parents and changes in career aspirations. One interesting aspect of this study is the communication difficulties that were due to English as a second language. Yet, this study does not focus on the demographic and cultural differences of the participants.

People's career development and goals are integrated with their family structure, histories, mentors, educational backgrounds, and values. All of these factors influence how a young person views the world of work, which ultimately has an impact on his or her preparations for the labor market and other adult roles (Flanagan, 1995; Steinberg, 1989). The choices that emerge, especially those that limit educational attainment, will profoundly affect the possibilities for job success and upward mobility over the life span (Topel & Ward, 1992). Conroy (1997) conducted an interdisciplinary study, drawing from the fields of vocational education, sociology/demography, and adolescent psychology, to identify the determinants of an adolescent's self-concept as related to future occupational self. Within her theoretical framework, young people form a personal template or identity prior to their actual entrance into the world of work. The social, family, and personal experiences interact with this image of the adolescent's future self. Conroy's study, which focused on career education, revealed that overall identity forms as a combination of family background, education, and socialization. Most research in this area has used the father's occupation and the mother's education, as well as the family's socioeconomic status as a frame of reference for predicting adolescent attainment, as related to the values and norms of the family's status (Blaue, 1992; Penick & Jepsen, 1992; Scott & Clark, 1986; Steinberg, 1989).

We also know, on the basis of social learning theory, the powerful influences provided by messages and ideas that influence people's cognitive development. According to Sharf (1996), Bandura's social learning tenets are formulated on the notion that humans are cognitive beings and learn by observing others. Part of his historical stance is based on the notion that people act according to possible consequences and repercussions of their actions rather than in reaction to the actual event. Therefore, children receive messages that support or thwart their thoughts about careers and vocations. Similarly, one's cultural upbringing also socially constructs a career narrative. Family and culture are intertwined, and to compartmentalize the two as separate risks missing the gestalt of a person's career story.

❧ Culture and Career Issues ❦

In our search of recent career research, we found a number of articles related to the impact of culture on career issues. Kerka (1998) identified the importance of context in career counseling and recommended the following:

1. Career counseling must take place within the cultural context, with counselors being aware of their own cultures.
2. Assumptions that all individuals in a culture have the same values, goals, and experiences should be avoided.
3. Race and ethnicity must be considered in interaction with gender and class.
4. The level of acculturation and stage of ethnic identity development should be identified.

The body of research integrating career and research on culture is complex, with endless possibilities arising out of multiple identities and complexities of individual differences. Throughout our study of the literature, common themes that emerge include career decision-making processes among ethnically diverse populations, career transitions and stability regarding gender, and research focusing on tools to address diverse populations.

Research on career decision making and perceived opportunity tends to focus on adult populations and the transmission of cultural values and experience. Lucero-Miller and Newman (1999) studied external factors such as ethnicity, acculturation level, and socioeconomic status that influence career indecision. Their conclusion was that career indecision is related to social and psychological variables affecting Mexican Americans. Another study focusing on Mexican Americans found high school girls' career expectations to be more influenced by culture than gender (McWhirter, Hackett, & Bandalos, 1998). Chung and Harmon (1999) evaluated the Perceived Occupational Opportunity Scale and Perceived Occupational Discrimination Scale with African Americans to increase the availability of cultural-appropriate career assessment tools. Although the study listed various limitations, the need for culturally sensitive career assessment tools emerged as an important consideration.

Another thread of research focuses on gender, ethnicity, and sexual orientation. Researchers looking at the career development of women and people of color have pointed out the strong influence of perceived barriers in the pursuit of career and educational goals. The larger social context of racism, sexism, and classism provides a backdrop with which to understand the continuing ability-attainment gap in the occupations of women and people of color. Yet, although a small number of studies have considered the effects of gender or ethnicity on perceived barriers, none have looked at both factors concurrently. This is an area that calls for closer examination, especially when one considers the profound combined impact of gender and ethnicity and the variations that occur across cultures (McWhirter, 1997). One study by Hernandez and Morales (1999) studied the narratives of Latina women in higher education. The women described the career experience as a road, and they also described career experiences including a limitation of duties, a lack of role models, and a glass-ceiling effect. These women used the metaphor to view career development as a journey with a mix of tribulations and success. Another study focusing on gender integrated the dimensions of gender, depression, and career among young adult women. Lucas, Skokowski, and Ancis (2000) found that females' difficulty with career decision was due to family relationships, family and culture, relationships with significant others and developmental and mental health issues.

Trusty, Robinson, and Plata (2000) studied the effects of gender, socioeconomic status, and early academic performance on postsecondary educational choice. Using longitudinal data, they found gender, academic performance, and socioeconomic status (in that order) to be strong indicators of academic choice in postsecondary education. A study focusing on gender and occupational aspirations among children found no significant differences regarding gender, gender role, and socioeconomic status (Sellers, Satcher, & Comas, 1999). The research on gender and career continues to identify the socialization of gender identity and its impact on career development. The research tends to support the notion that there are more limitations for females than for males. Such issues as equal pay, mentoring, and access to promotion continue to be areas of research. McWhirter (1997), in a study of 1,139 Mexican American and European American high school students, found that female participants and Mexican American participants anticipated more barriers than their European American counterparts. She suggested that her results are consistent with other studies (Arbona, 1990; Lent, Brown, & Hackett, 1994) that indicate that there are ethnic and gender differences in perceived barriers to educational and career goal attainment.

Sexual orientation and career issues are related to career, family experiences, and cultural identity. Career development, work experiences, and attitudes in relation to sexual orientation are discussed in the literature. Mobley and Slaney (1996) identified the relevance of Holland's career theory with gay and lesbian identity issues. Similarly, Dunkle (1996) integrated Super's life-span approach with gay and lesbian identity research. Research literature also includes discrimination, career decision making, and influences on relational issues. There is less literature studying the experiences of transgender individuals and the impact of layered identities.

One cannot focus on ethnicity, race, and gender without noting the integration of socioeconomic class. Rothenberg (1992) found that being female and of color greatly increases one's chances of being poor. Most of the research related to socioeconomic status and career is based on vocational literature, including welfare-to-work initiatives. Kincheloe (1999) studied the impact of class issues on work and career. Believing in a strong work ethic and dreaming of economic success were corner-stones of early America. Yet, today, he noted that most new wealth in the 1980s and 1990s did not come from long work hours but from "instant wealth" through investments and dividends. So the belief that economic success is guaranteed if someone simply works hard and is determined is a misnomer. Kincheloe (1999) stated, "The connection between class position and one's willingness to work may be less direct than many Americans have assumed" (p. 144). The lack of research in the area of class issues and career stems from the complexity of class dynamics. Yet, we know that family upbringing influences one's views and class expe-riences, including perceived career limitations and expectations.

One variable of a person's contextual influence that is not well doc-umented is that of spiritual and religious influences. The research that exists focuses on the influence of religious and spiritual issues on career decision making, especially with young adults. Trusty and Watts (1999) found a positive, yet weak relationship between religious perceptions and life/career outlook. There is a need to further develop our under-standing of the religious and spiritual issues related to career.

Nevertheless, we know that culture and family both play an influ-ential role in career decisions. The importance of describing and imple-menting research that addresses the complexity of career counseling must be included.

◆ The Convergence of Family, Culture, and Career ◆

To date, there has been little research that intentionally integrates fam-ily, culture, and career. The current research that addresses such topics tends be about family and couple issues within a culture. For example, Chi-Chung (1995) studied the life cycle and career salience on work–family issues with a population from Singapore and found that men were more career oriented than women and that women tended to place family and marriage higher than career, at least in early adulthood. Another study by Bharat (1995) found that Indian working couples' atti-tudes toward employed women is influenced by the women's career status. Attitudes toward professional employment roles for women were found to be more positive than toward nonprofessional roles. Yet, sex roles within the couples relationship remained the same regardless of career status. Although these two examples are a beginning, the researchers did not equally attend to both family and culture. The research tended to focus on family within the context of ethnicity rather than the convergence of family and ethnicity.

The lack of research focusing on the complexities and interaction of career, family, and ethnicity is not simply an issue of career study but also of social advocacy. Herr and Niles (1998) stated that the field of career counseling needs to emphasize the following: (a) Neither the counselor nor the client's problems exist within a vacuum; (b) most problems a client brings are multidimensional; therefore, a counselor's tools must be multidimensional; and (c) career counseling is a sociopolitical instrument. As researchers, we need to be able to study the complexities of internal and external influences. The study of career needs to occur from a multidimensional stance and a lens that realizes the societal impact of career counseling and research. As a profession, we need to ask if we are studying career counseling from a multidimensional view. Are we taking into consideration the complexities of individuals and the multiplicity of identities individuals possess? To more clearly illustrate the current research in these areas, we summarize the strengths and limitations that we found.

❧ Strengths ❦

A review of current research reveals increasing attention to diverse populations, including racial/ethnic minorities and people with disabilities (Arbona, 2000). For example, Enright, Conyers, and Szymanski (1996) examined the impact of career counselors on perpetuating the misconceptions of college students with disabilities. Other researchers have focused on career issues of specific populations (Bharat, 1995; Stead, 1996). For example, Lucero-Miller and Newman (1999) studied a sample of Mexican American college students who may be highly acculturated, and Hernandez and Morales (1999) looked at the developmental experiences of Latinas working in higher education.

A substantial amount of research has been conducted on issues around gender and women's career sequencing (Stone & McKee, 2000; Wentling, 1996; Zhang & Farley, 1995). A limited amount of research has also looked at the effects of gender within the context of family, culture, and career (Betz, 1992). A recent example is a study by Mayo and Christenfeld (1999) that investigated career patterns of women minorities and their own performance expectations. Most studies, however, seem to gravitate to the work–family interface, especially as this relates to the changing roles of women in society (Chi-Chung, 1995). Research in this area has generated studies that focus on dual-career couples, gender roles, balance, and efficacy (Beutell, 1996; Stolts-Loike, 1992). For example, Burley (1995) compared the hours of family-related duties between men and women as affecting work–family conflict and marital satisfaction. Miller, Campbell, and Morrison (2000) studied the role of spousal support on work satisfaction and stress; and Nesbitt (1995) looked at the role of family support on clergy.

Another area of substantial investigation includes family-of-origin influences. Although historically most research in this area focuses on factors affecting specific vocational preferences, newer studies in this area have investigated how families can actually facilitate career development (Blustein, 1994; Penick & Jepsen, 1992). Parental influence on career has been a specific focus within the literature (Guerra & Braungart-Rieker, 1999; Helwig & Myrin, 1997; Young, Paseluikho, & Valach, 1997).

Research in the area of vocational interests, which began in the early 1900s, is extensive. The changing social context warrants further studies, however, especially as interests relate to the career development of women, racial/ethnic minorities, and older adults. Much research indicates that values also have a profound influence on career-life decisions and work adjustment (Dawis & Lofquist, 1984). While much has been done regarding the impact of values on career development, an increased understanding is called for regarding differences in values in light of gender and ethnicity (Niles & Goodnough, 1996).

A careful review of the literature reveals a growing recognition of the importance of family dynamics and culture on career (Larson & Wilson, 1998; Nesbitt, 1995). A major strength of recent research is the development of newer, contextual models that address the interrelated aspects of culture, family, and career (McWhirter et al., 1998; Ponterotto, Rivera, & Sueyoshi, 2000). The fundamental worldview shared by these models incorporates a number of factors influencing the dynamic and evolving relationship between an individual and the environment. Overall, however, the current strengths of the literature could be better described as a movement toward increased attention to the combined influence of culture and family on career development.

❧ Limitations ❦

Although the current body of research reflects a trend toward looking at social, cultural, and environmental factors, large gaps remain. Few researchers have investigated specialized populations, for example, gays, lesbians, and older adults. Some factors influencing career development have not been investigated in any way, such as the role of the family and close relationships within the context of culture. Larger societal issues are lacking in the literature as well, especially as to the impact of sexism, racism, and social barriers on career opportunities (Blustein, 1994). There has also been little research addressing the role of personality in career outcomes. This is a crucial gap in the literature, especially as personality relates to other domains of career-related behavior, job satisfaction, and career success (Seibert & Kraimer, 2001).

Although variables in each of the areas of family, culture, and career are represented to varying degrees in the literature, our review reflects a general lack of integration of the three areas. Many studies report on the interests of researchers from different disciplines, yet few findings have been unified into the mainstream of career development research (Vondracek & Fouad, 1994). This has been compounded by the fact that most studies tend to report findings on small samples of specific populations, which cannot be generalized to other groups. A related limitation of the research reviewed is an overall lack of studies conducted on large and diverse populations. Additionally, most of the research is descriptive in nature rather than process oriented, which compromises the complex interaction of multiple variables on a person's career. We also noticed that researchers have neglected the sociopolitical aspects of career counseling by not addressing the issue at all. Although the contextual–developmental frameworks approach an evolving social context, few have been translated into practice. In addition, the lack of longitudinal studies discounts the need to take into account environmental fluctuations and historical change (Vondracek & Fouad, 1994). A potentially powerful model in the literature has not yet been realized. Although some studies are now being replicated, most seem to reflect the societal value of quick, simple solutions over more complex and time-consuming models.

❧ What Is Needed? ❧

It is tempting to begin this section by answering with a simple, "Everything." The many articles described earlier in this chapter usually addressed one or two dimensions and used the others, if at all, to specify demographics of the studied population. We are suggesting that future research explicitly address the three components of career, family, and culture—designing studies for the purpose with all three factors in mind from the beginning. For example, one could study how birth order affects career maturity of African American teenagers, or more specifically, teenage girls. One could research how dual-career lesbian couples navigate their transition to retirement or the opportunities one has for a promotion that would mean moving to another city or country. The possibilities are limitless.

In a passionate article about the interface of work and relationships, Blustein (2001) stated, "Indeed, the interface between work and interpersonal relationships remains a relatively unexplored frontier in our search for a broad and contextually rich understanding of human behavior and its various manifestations" (pp. 179-180). Although addressing only two aspects of our triad, he presented a short list of next steps that seem to us to apply equally well to our challenge: "(a) What are the predictable ways in which these domains intersect? (b) What are the theoretical and conceptual frameworks that might be useful in conceptualizing this intersection? And (c) what sorts of methods might be useful to further explore these questions?"

Shultiess, Kress, Manzi, and Glassock (2001) identified a number of areas for further investigation. Although their focus is the role of relationships in career development, they recognized that cultural factors need to be included in that research. They suggested that inquiry is needed into the interaction of relationships and career development across developmental levels and with "an array of populations across the demographic boundaries of age, gender, racial/ethnic background and social class" (p. 237). They also identified the areas of family composition and available support as meriting further study. Although parental influences on teens, for example, have been studied extensively, the role of siblings and other relatives is less known. Furthermore, Shultiess et al. pointed out that even when we as researchers identify sources of support, for example, we often do not know as much as we could about how these operate to assist or hinder career development.

In discussing relational issues in career development, Shultiess et al. (2001) made a strong case for using qualitative research in investigating these connections. They stated, "the context within which our deepest connections occur can no longer be ignored. Culture, age, socioeconomic background, and family structure must be attended to as we attempt to identify the role that relationships play as careers unfold" (p. 215). One barrier to such integrated research is a still pervasive counseling assumption that values individual autonomy and an internal locus of control. As Toporek (2000) stated, "Cultural values such as independence, self-sufficiency, and personal responsibility have shaped the ways we have been trained to view client problems and provide interventions and treatment" (p. 11). If we shape our interventions from an individualistic point of view, we usually shape our research from the same perspective. We are suggesting here that other perspectives also be included—those that combine inquiry into individual career development with inquiry in the effects of family and culture on that individual.

To further illustrate this concept, we have created a matrix (see Table 7.1). A sample list of dimensions is provided in each column: family, culture, and career. (Note that this is meant to be a sampler, not an exhaustive list.)

In planning research that integrates the three dimensions, one would then pick a dimension from the family column, one from the culture column, and one from the career column. So, one could investigate the relationship among dual-career issues, ethnicity, and decision-making or dual-career issues, gender, and aspirations, and so forth. Each of these dimensions could also, of course, have subdimensions to be explored. Thus, one could look into the way that birth order affected the values of

Table 7.1

Sample List of Dimensions of Family, Culture, and Career

Family	Culture	Career
Dual career	Ethnicity	Decision making
Birth order	Gender	Transitions
Parental influence	Age	Aspirations
Gender roles	Social class	Values
Family history	Sexual orientation	Interests
Conflict/balance	Disabilities	Knowledge of opportunities

people with hidden disabilities, or Asians, or Asian/Pacific Islanders. Furthermore, one could look into combinations of one or more dimensions within a column related to dimensions in each of the others. Thus, a researcher could collect data on parental influences of female teens' interests and decision-making style. As stated before, the possibilities are limitless. Students interested in this area should find no shortage of dissertation topics!

Ultimately, the goal is to provide career research that encompasses the complexities and intricacies of a diverse society. The ability of the career counselor to draw from effective therapeutic tools, career developmental models, and assessment instruments based on solid contextual research is an important key to the future of career counseling. During the last few years, we have seen an increase in the number of studies addressing culture and family. The next step is to integrate these variables to promote effective and ethical career counseling. The fluid out-of-the-box model is a first step to begin conceptualizing career counseling and career research by viewing individuals as complex and in context.

❧ Summary ❧

Ultimately, the goal is to provide career research that encompasses the complexities and intricacies of a diverse society. The ability of the career counselor to draw from effective therapeutic tools, career developmental models, and assessment instruments based on solid contextual research is an important key to the future of career counseling. During the last few years, we have seen an increase in the number of studies addressing culture and family. The next step is to integrate these variables to promote effective and ethical career counseling. The fluid out-of-the-box model is a first step to begin conceptualizing career counseling and career research by viewing individuals as complex and in context.

࿚ References ࿚

Amudson, N., & Penner, K. (1998). Parent involved career exploration. *Career Development Quarterly, 47,* 135-144.

Arbona, C. (1990). Career counseling research and Hispanics: A review of the literature. *The Career Psychologist, 18,* 300-323.

Arbona, C. (2000). Practice and research in career counseling and development. *Career Development Quarterly, 49,* 98-134.

Betz, N. E. (1992). Counseling uses of career efficacy. *Career Development Quarterly, 41,* 22-26.

Betz, N. E., & Fitzgerald, L. (1987). *The career psychology of women.* Orlando, FL: Academic Press.

Beutell, N. J. (1996). Work and family variables, entrepreneurial career success and psychological well-being. *Journal of Vocational Behavior, 48,* 275-300.

Bharat, S. (1995). Attitudes and sex-role perceptions among working couples in India. *Journal of Comparative Family Studies, 26,* 371-388.

Blaue, P. (1992). Mobility and status attainment. *Contemporary Sociology, 21,* 596-598.

Blustein, D. (1994). "Who am I?": The questions of self and identity in career development. In M. L. Savicksas & R. W. Lent (Eds.), *Convergence in career development theories: Implications for science and practice* (pp. 139-154). Palo Alto, CA: Consulting Psychologists Press.

Blustein, D. L. (2001). The interface of work and relationships: Critical knowledge for 21st century psychology. *Counseling Psychologist, 29,* 179-192.

Brown, D., Brooks, L., & Associates. (1996). *Career: Choice and development* (3rd ed.). San Francisco: Jossey-Bass.

Burley, K. (1995). Family variables as mediators of the relationship between work-family conflict and marital adjustment among dual-career men and women. *Journal of Social Psychology, 135,* 483-497.

Chi-Chung, Y. (1995). The effects of career salience and life-cycle variables on perceptions of work-family interfaces. *Human Relations, 48,* 265-284.

Chung, Y., & Harmon, L. W. (1999). Assessment of perceived occupational opportunity for Black Americans. *Career Assessment, 7,* 45-62.

Conroy, C. (1997). Influences on career choice of rural youth and resulting implications for career development programming: When job awareness and exploration are not enough. *Journal of Vocational Education and Research, 22,* 3-19.

Dawis, R. V., & Lofquist, L. H. (1984). *A psychological theory of work adjustment.* Minneapolis: University of Minnesota Press.

Dunkle, J. H. (1996). Toward an integration of gay and lesbian identity development and Super's life-span approach. *Journal of Vocational Behavior, 48,* 149-159.

Enright, M. S., Conyers, L. M., & Szymanski, E. (1996). Career and career-related educational concerns of college students with disabilities. *Journal of Counseling & Development, 75,* 103-152.

Evans, K. M., & Rotter, J. C. (2000). Multicultural family approaches to career counseling. *The Family Journal, 8,* 67-71.

Flanagan, C. (1995). Reframing concepts of development in the context of social change. In P. Noack, M. Hofer, & J. Youniss (Eds.), *Psychological responses to social change* (pp. 23–35). New York: Walter DeGruyter.

Guerra, A., & Braungart-Rieker, J. (1999). Predicting career indecision in college students: The roles of identity formation and parental relationship factors. *Career Development Quarterly, 47,* 255–266.

Helwig, A., & Myrin, M. (1997). Ten-year stability of Holland codes within one family. *Career Development Quarterly, 46,* 62–71.

Hernandez, T. J., & Morales, N. E. (1999). Career, culture, and compromise: Career development experiences of Latinas working in higher education. *Career Development Quarterly, 48,* 45–58.

Herr, E., & Niles, S. (1998). From multiculturalism to social action. In C. Lee & G. Walz (Eds.), *Social action: A mandate for counselors* (pp. 117–136). Alexandria, VA: American Counseling Association and ERIC Counseling & Student Services Clearing House.

Kerka, S. (1998). *Career development and gender, race, and class* (Report No. EDO-CE-98-199). Washington, DC: Office of Educational Research and Improvement. (ERIC Document Reproduction Service No. ED 421 641).

Kincheloe, J. (1999). *How do we tell the workers?* Boulder, CO: Westview Press.

Larson, J., & Wilson, S. (1998). Family of origin influences on young adult career decision problems: A test of Bowenian theory. *American Journal of Family Therapy, 26,* 39–53.

Lent, R. W., Brown, S. D., & Hackett, G. (1994). Toward a unifying social cognitive theory of career and academic interest, choice, and performance. *Journal of Vocational Behavior, 45,* 79–122.

Lewis, J., & Arnold, M. (1998). From multiculturalism to social action. In C. Lee & G. Walz (Eds.), *Social action: A mandate for counselors* (pp. 51–66). Alexandria, VA: American Counseling Association and ERIC Counseling & Student Services Clearing House.

Lucas, M., Skokowski, C. T., & Ancis, J. R. (2000). Contextual themes in career decision making of female clients who indicate depression. *Journal of Counseling & Development, 78,* 316–325.

Lucero-Miller, D., & Newman, J. L. (1999). Predicting acculturation using career, family and demographic variables in a sample of Mexican American students. *Journal of Multicultural Counseling and Development, 27,* 75–92.

Mayo, M., & Christenfeld, N. (1999). Gender, race, and performance expectations of college students. *Journal of Multicultural Counseling, 27,* 93–94.

McWhirter, E. H. (1997). Perceived barriers to education and career: Ethnic and gender differences. *Journal of Vocational Behavior, 50,* 124–140.

McWhirter, E. H., Hackett, G., & Bandalos, D. L. (1998). A casual model of educational plans and career expectations of Mexican American high school girls. *Journal of Counseling Psychology, 45,* 166–181.

Miller, D., Campbell, M., & Morrison, C. (2000). Work and family: Satisfaction, stress and spousal support. *Journal of Employment Counseling, 37,* 35–40.

Mobley, M., & Slaney, R. B. (1996). Holland's theory: Its relevance for lesbian women and gay men. *Journal of Vocational Behavior, 48,* 125–135.

Nesbitt, P. (1995). Marriage, parenthood, and the ministry: Differential effects of marriage and family on male and female clergy careers. *Sociology of Religion, 56,* 397-415.

Niles, S., & Goodnough, G. (1996). Life-role salience and values: A review of recent research. *Career Development Quarterly, 45,* 65-86.

Penick N., & Jepsen, D. (1992). Family functioning and adolescent career development. *Career Development Quarterly, 40,* 208-222.

Phillips, S., Christopher-Sisk, E., & Gravino, K. (2001). Making career decisions in a relational context. *Counseling Psychologist, 29,* 193-213.

Phillips-Miller, D., Campbell, N., & Morrison, C. (2000). Work and family: Satisfaction, stress, and spousal support. *Journal of Employment Counseling, 37,* 16-30.

Ponterotto, J., Rivera, L., & Sueyoshi, L. (2000). The career-in-culture interview: A semi-structured protocol for the cross-cultural intake interview. *Career Development Quarterly, 49,* 85-92.

Rothenberg, P. S. (1992). *Race, class and gender: An integrated study.* New York: St. Martin's Press.

Scott, D., & Clark, M. (1986). The school experiences of Black girls: The interaction of gender, race, and socioeconomic status. *Phi Delta Kappan, 67,* 520-526.

Seibert, S. E., & Kraimer, M. L. (2001). The five-factor model of personality and career success. *Journal of Vocational Behavior, 45,* 1-21.

Sellers, N., Satcher, J., & Comas, R. (1999). Children's occupational aspirations: Comparisons by gender, gender role identity, and socioeconomic status. *Professional School Counseling, 2,* 314-317.

Sharf, R. S. (1996). *Theories of psychotherapy and counseling.* Pacific Grove, CA: Brooks/Cole.

Shultiess, D. C. P., Kress, H. M., Manzi, A. J., & Glassock, J. M. J. (2001). Relational influence in career development: A qualitative inquiry. *Counseling Psychologist, 29,* 214-239.

Sinacore, A. L., & Akcali, F. (2000). Men in families: Job satisfaction and self-esteem. *Journal of Career and Development, 27,* 1-13.

Stead, G. (1996). Career development of Black South African adolescents: A developmental-contextual perspective. *Journal of Counseling & Development, 74,* 270-275.

Steinberg, L. (1989). *Adolescence* (2nd ed.). New York: Alfred A. Knopf.

Stolts-Loike, M. (1992). The working family: Helping women balance the roles of wife, mother, and career woman. *Career Development Quarterly, 40,* 244-256.

Stone, L., & McKee, N. (2000). Gendered futures: Student visions of career and family on a college campus. *Anthropology and Education Quarterly, 31,* 67-89.

Topel, R., & Ward, M. (1992). Job mobility and the careers of young men. *Quarterly of Economics, 107,* 439-479.

Toporek, R. L. (2000). Developing a common language and framework for understanding advocacy in counseling. In J. Lewis & L. Bradley (Eds.), *Advocacy in counseling* (pp. 1-16). Greensboro, NC: Caps Publications.

Trusty, J., Robinson, C. R., & Plata, M. (2000). Effects of gender, socioeconomic status, and early academic performance on postsecondary educational choice. *Journal of Counseling and Development, 78,* 463–472.

Trusty, J., & Watts, R. (1999). Relationship of high school seniors' religious perceptions and behavior to educational, career, and leisure variables. *Counseling and Values, 44,* 30–39.

Vondracek F., & Fouad, N. (1994). Developmental contextualism: An integrative framework. In M. Savickas & R. Lent (Eds.), *Convergence in career development theories* (pp. 207–214). Palo Alto, CA: Consulting Psychologists Press.

Wentling, R. M. (1996). A study of the career development and aspirations of women in middle management. *Human Resource Development Quarterly, 7,* 253–270.

Young, R., Paseluikho, M., & Valach, L. (1997). The role of emotion in the construction of career in parent–adolescent conversations. *Journal of Counseling and Development, 76,* 36–44.

Zhang, C., & Farley, J. (1995). Gender and the distribution of household work: A comparison of self-reports by female college faculty in the United States and China. *Journal of Comparative Family Studies, 26,* 195–205.

❧ Chapter 8 ❧

Integration of Counseling Standards

Marty Jencius

When one looks at ethical guidelines for practicing counselors regarding culture, family, and career, the task is complicated by the multiple ethical codes, standards of practice, and counseling competencies that related professional organizations maintain. This chapter takes a two-tiered approach to looking at counseling standards: *practice* and *training*. The first tier examines ethical codes and competencies established by the subspecialties covered in this book. Ethical codes and competencies are reflective of what is considered sound *practice*. Historically, counseling associations have been using codes of ethics before establishing training standards. The second tier looks at *training* standards, specifically those established by the Council for Accreditation of Counseling and Related Educational Programs (CACREP).

Reflective of the subject of this book, counselors and counselor educators would need to look at three American Counseling Association (ACA) divisions in addition to the *ACA Code of Ethics and Standards of Practice*. The ACA divisions reflective of practice in the area of culture, family, and career are, respectively, the Association for Multicultural Counseling and Development (AMCD), the International Association of Marriage and Family Counselors (IAMFC), and the National Career Development Association (NCDA). Without going into the historic development of these divisions, suffice it to say that these divisions are where counselors and counselor educators turn for direction in these specialty areas. These codes reflect the ethically sound practice of a counselor working with culturally diverse clients facing career issues.

The program of study the counselor obtains lays the groundwork for sound practice. In judging the adequacy of preparation, the leading accrediting body for counselor programs in the United States is CACREP. CACREP provides program objectives in the areas of culture (Social and Cultural Diversity), family (through their separate program accreditation for Marital, Couple, and Family Counseling/Therapy), and career (through their separate program accreditation for Career Counseling). By looking at the program preparation in these areas, one can gain insight into responsive methods of teaching essential sound practice.

❧ Ethical Codes ❦

Given that each of the mentioned ACA divisions is affiliated with ACA, members are expected to abide by the *ACA Code of Ethics and Standards of Practice*. In addition to the *ACA Code of Ethics and Standards of Practice*, each division addresses its special needs through (a) divisional ethical codes, (b) divisional standards of practice, (c) divisional competencies, or some combination of the three.

AMCD

The Association for Multicultural Counseling and Development's (AMCD) Multicultural Counseling Competencies (MCC; Arredondo et al., 1996a) resulted from a professional call for action by Sue, Arredondo, and McDavis (1992) and the development of the MCC. AMCD's Professional Standards Committee of 1994–1995 worked to complete the operationalization of the competencies (Arredondo et al., 1996b). *The Operationalization of the Multicultural Counseling Competencies* (Arredondo et al., 1996a, 1996b) takes into consideration other reference tools, including the Personal Dimensions of Identity model (Arredondo & Glauner, 1992), and continues to look at the various competencies and suggests strategies to achieve the competencies and objectives.

The MCC is organized into two intersecting domains. The first domain attempts to capture the range of a counselor's awareness from internalized cultural values to the client's worldview to the interaction of those two dimensions into intervention strategies. The second range of domains is that of attitudes and beliefs, knowledge, and skills present for each of the three dimensions of the first domain. The dimensions in the second domain add a developmental focus to the education of the multiculturally competent counselor. The attitudes and beliefs dimension focuses on what inherent beliefs the counselor holds about other cultures and how they might differ from other cultures. The knowledge dimension focuses on the acquisition of knowledge about a culture beyond the counselor's personal belief system. The skill dimension focuses on the application of knowledge gained from the counselor's exploration. Previous success in the attitude and belief dimension ("what I hold as personal truths about culture") and the knowledge dimension ("what I now know is truth about a culture") is essential for success in the skills dimension ("how I apply the truths when working with this client/culture"). The developmental aspect of this domain is further important to how one organizes thinking about a combination of codes from other disciplines.

Of the three areas addressed by the book—culture, career, and family—cultural competencies become central to the various codes. The MCC covers the scope of beliefs and behaviors that counselors need to acquire to be successful as transcultural counselors. Each of the competencies functions to address a particular aspect of multicultural awareness: understanding of racism, indigenous healing methods, communicating the value of bilingualism, and so on. Each of these competencies addresses the attitudes and beliefs, knowledge, and skills that a counselor needs to be considered multiculturally competent.

The MCC authors suggest the usefulness of extending these codes specifically to other counseling subdisciplines. Noted in the supportive literature of the MCC is an apparent call to action to address needs into other areas (Arredondo et al., 1996a): "For areas of assessment, evaluation, research, career guidance and other counseling applications, additional competencies need to be developed with a multicultural focus" (p. 45).

As ethical codes and standards of ACA divisions go through periodic revision, there is more attention paid to diversity competencies. For a good example, see the Association for Specialists in Group Work (ASGW, 1998) *Principles for Diversity-Competent Group Workers*. In this case, ASGW has used the framework of the MCC, including major heading sections of counselor awareness of his or her own cultural values and beliefs, awareness of the client's worldview, and culturally appropriate interventions skills. Each of these larger domains is further examined from the counselor's beliefs and attitudes, knowledge, and skills. As one will see when looking at the extension of the MCC to the other dimensions explored by this book (career and family), continued effort to be directly inclusive by professional organizations needs to occur.

IAMFC

The International Association of Marriage and Family Counselors (IAMFC, 2001) has recently updated their Ethical Codes. The code is divided into eight sections: client well-being, confidentiality, competence, assessment, private practice, research and publications, supervision, and media and public statements. These eight sections are meant to parallel the eight sections found in the ACA Code of Ethics. IAMFC Ethical Codes are meant to supplement the ACA Code of Ethics, and their members are encouraged to abide by the parent organization's ethical code.

In looking for convergence of other codes within the IAMFC Ethical Codes, IAMFC makes a global statement about recognizing other worldviews and how its members should abide by the AMCD Multicultural Counseling Competencies.

> Members recognize the influence of worldview and cultural factors (race, ethnicity, gender, social class, spirituality, sexual orientation, educational status) on the presenting problem, family functioning, and problem-solving skills. Counselors are aware of indigenous healing practices and incorporate them into treatment when necessary or feasible. Members are encouraged to follow the guidelines provided in Multicultural Competencies.

This endorsement for following the Multicultural Competencies leaves a wide margin or discretion to the member, instead of tying cultural competencies directly in the code. In the most critical sense, this globally supports the following of the Multicultural Competencies as an add-on to IAMFC Ethical Codes, at the same time seeing the IAMFC Ethical Codes as augmenting the ACA Code of Ethics.

Beyond the global statement mentioned above, the IAMFC Ethical Codes also include a few statements directed to diversity issues. The first statement reflects respecting diversity within the framework of the family.

> They strive to respect the diversity of personal attributes and do not stereotype or force families into prescribed attitudes, roles, or behaviors.

This would include being sensitive to the needs of extended family issues and single-parent families. The emphasis with this statement is appreciating the ideographic nature of the family from a within-family differences point of view.

A second IAMFC Ethical Codes statement takes a systemic, group differences viewpoint of diversity, and in such parallels the cultural–historic dimension presented by McFadden (1999) in the stylistic model of transcultural counseling.

> Members do not discriminate on the basis of race, gender, social class, disability, spirituality, religion, age, sexual orientation, nationality, language, educational level, marital status, or political affiliation.

This statement covers acceptance of differences based on the cultural–historic level of the stylistic model, accepting the significance of how nationality, race, and ethnic group developed in the client historically. This ethical code holds that marriage and family counselors need to be aware of the impact of these intrinsic issues with clients. That is, when clients enter a counseling relationship, they bring these dimensions with them and the counselor should not discriminate on the basis of these qualities.

The IAMFC Ethical Codes challenge a member to develop cultural competency beyond the earlier mentioned global statement regarding accepting worldview. In the following statement, the three levels of competency endorsed by AMCD—awareness (attitudes and beliefs), knowledge, and skills—are mentioned directly as areas of development.

> Members are committed to gaining cultural competency, including awareness, knowledge, and skills to work with a diverse clientele. Members are aware of their own biases, values, and assumptions about human behavior. They employ techniques/assessment strategies that are appropriate for dealing with diverse cultural groups.

Beyond this statement, IAMFC could only seek to directly align their Ethical Codes directly with AMCD competencies. This would entitle a fusion of ethical standards later described in this chapter as convergent codes.

The concept of a commitment to gaining cultural competency is extended beyond the individual member to the area of marriage and family counselor supervision. The IAMFC Ethical Codes call for a supervisory member to be aware of how cultural issues can influence the supervisory process.

> Members understand the influence of cultural issues in the supervisory relationship, including issues of oppression and power structures within the relationship.

Because the supervisory process can inherently contain a power structure of supervisor over supervisee, a pairing of members of two different cultures during supervision may also historically represent this dynamic. The outcome of such parings, considering a client of a different culture, is a multiple possible worldview position held by the client, counselor, and supervisor. The supervisory triad becomes further extended because of the multiple possible worldviews (Brown & Landrum-Brown, 1995). IAMFC member supervisors need to look at the additional layer of cultural differences between the supervisor and supervisee. This level of cultural awareness between the supervisor and supervisee is extended appropriately to include the supervisee and the client.

> Members who provide supervision discuss cultural issues in the work of supervisees and clients, and promote cultural sensitivity and competence in the supervisees.

IAMFC has included this code as a way of establishing supervisors' need to address their cultural competence when working with clients. The code establishes a process that supports supervisors gaining cultural competency, perhaps through their own supervision, and passing it on to their supervisees.

Finally, IAMFC takes a position in their Ethical Codes with regard to assessment and culturally diverse clients. As stated in the IAMFC Ethical Codes, marriage and family counselors see the family as their client and should not misinterpret behaviors in the family that are consistent with their cultural origin but that may be viewed by unfamiliar counselors as a symptom of some greater pathology.

> Family counselors should be cautious when assessing culturally diverse clients. Family counselors include cultural factors when assessing behaviors, functioning, and presenting symptoms of clients. Counselors are careful to use assessment techniques that have been appropriately formed and standardized on diverse populations. Counselors are also careful to interpret results from standardized assessment instruments in light of cultural factors.

Furthermore, when using standardized assessments, marriage and family therapists are encouraged to only use those instruments that have been normed for diverse populations. Counselors often need to consider the client's cultural worldview when reading the results of such assessments.

NCDA

The National Career Development Association's (NCDA, 2000b) Ethical Standards address fewer of the cultural issues than does IAMFC. Primarily, NCDA's Ethical Standards look at global issues when it comes to dealing with diversity in their clientele. NCDA encourages members to be aware of their own biases and the impact that racial stereotyping can have on helping clients make career decisions. By becoming aware of discrimination, career counselors can guard the personal rights of clients.

> NCDA members avoid bringing their personal or professional issues into the counseling relationship. Through an awareness of the impact of stereotyping and discrimination (e.g., biases based on age, disability, ethnicity, gender, race, religion, or sexual preference), career counselors guard the individual rights and personal dignity of the client in the counseling relationship.

NCDA, like IAMFC, has made this general statement to blanket behaviors that counselors can exhibit that discriminate against clients.

With regard to the AMCD Multicultural Counseling Competencies, NCDA has only responded to one dimension of awareness. With this statement, NCDA's code does not extend itself to include knowledge and skill dimensions of counseling competencies.

Another ethical code calls career counselors to gain knowledge in other cultures if they are not familiar with the culture.

> NCDA members who counsel clients from cultures different from their own must gain knowledge, personal awareness, and sensitivity pertinent to the client populations served and must incorporate culturally relevant techniques into their practice.

The code also describes the need for the counselor to gain personal awareness (one of the dimensions of AMCD's Multicultural Counseling Competencies) but does not offer a vehicle for such personal awareness. In addition, career counselors are to incorporate culturally relevant techniques in their practice (another of AMCD's Multicultural Counseling Competencies) without describing methods to obtain training in such techniques. This last code seems to streamline the process of cultural awareness and does not give room to consider the effort involved in becoming a culturally competent counselor.

Similar to the IAMFC Ethical Codes, the NCDA Ethical Standards caution its members from using assessment measures that are not appropriate for minorities who are not represented in the norms of the measure.

> NCDA members must proceed with caution when attempting to evaluate and interpret performances of minority group members or other persons who are not represented in the norm group on which the instrument was standardized.

NCDA recognizes that practitioners use assessments as a means to determine clients' interests, work values, and skills. The NCDA Ethical Standards ask that counselors be sensitive about applying assessments to persons who are not represented in the instrument's norm group. The literature provides many examples of bias in testing, much related to the pursuit of career (Carter & Swanson, 1990). Even with the advent of culture-specific testing, work needs to be done to bring assessment up to a culture-fair status. (For a further discussion of this topic, see chapter 3 in this book.)

NCDA has established revised 1997 Career Counseling Competencies that cover a variety of minimal competencies and also cover performance indicators (National Career Development Association, 2000a). The minimal competency states, "knowledge and skills considered essential in providing career counseling and development processes to diverse populations." The performance indicators further define this minimal competency into skills associated with diverse clientele. Performance indicators regarding diverse populations include the following:

1. Identify developmental models and multicultural counseling competencies.
2. Identify developmental needs unique to various diverse populations, including those of different gender, sexual orientation, ethnic group, race, and physical or mental capacity.
3. Define career development programs to accommodate needs unique to various diverse populations.
4. Find appropriate methods or resources to communicate with limited-English-proficient individuals.
5. Identify alternative approaches to meet career-planning needs for individuals of various diverse populations.
6. Identify community resources and establish linkages to assist clients with specific needs.
7. Assist other staff members, professionals, and community members in understanding the unique needs/characteristics of diverse populations with regard to career exploration, employment expectations, and economic/social issues.
8. Advocate for the career development and employment of diverse populations.
9. Design and deliver career development programs and materials to hard-to-reach populations. (NCDA, 2000a)

These performance indicators are in the spirit of creating a culturally competent career counselor. Many of the above performance indicators describe an outcome and do not address the skill development process the counselor had to obtain to be able to perform successfully and create such an outcome.

❧ Interpreting Multiple Codes in a Single Context ❧

The difficult task for the counselor working with culture, family, and career is to sort through the ethical codes to establish an awareness and then a working knowledge of these codes. Generally, this means that a counselor needs to independently be aware of each association's ethical codes and attempts to abide by each one in a separate context. With multiple associations, each having its own set of standards, in some cases complementary and in some cases conflictual, counselors are often left to choose the code that applies within their own current context. When culture surfaces as the issue, the counselor thinks in terms of codes related to culture. The context of the counselor–client relationship may shift to focus on family issues, at which point the counselor is drawn into the codes that reflect the family as the client. Should life-span career issues become prominent within the family, codes related to career counseling take precedence. This difficult process seems to be a linear interpretation of ethical codes based on the presenting issues at hand.

A *linear interpretation* of ethical codes is an additive process whereby a counselor who first defines his or her work as a counselor may look to an umbrella association like the ACA for its listing of Ethical Codes and Standards of Practice. Given that the counselor has a sound understanding of the ACA codes, when faced with a client who is from a different culture, the counselor may seek better understanding by looking at the AMCD Multicultural Counseling Competencies. At this point, the counselor may vacillate between what they abide by in the ACA Code and their own understanding of the cultural issues based on where they are in their own cultural development. Add to the mix the additional dimension of the client's family, and now the counselor finds himself or herself trying to simultaneously address the issues found in IAMFC Ethical Codes. This becomes further complicated when the issue turns to career issues, and now the counselor has to look at NCDA Ethical Standards. In this scenario, the counselor is chasing the client with the associated ethical standard at the time. The interaction has a singular linear feel to it as the counselor works with the client on one dimension at a time.

Another style for addressing multiple applications of ethical codes to one client or family is to look at the interaction of the codes with each other. To find that interaction, look at where the codes complement each other and at which point they diverge from each other. An *interactive interpretation* of the code occurs when one code clearly stipulates actions intended to foster the development of conditions described in another code. We have suggested in the above discussion where the AMCD Multicultural Counseling Competencies and the IAMFC Ethical Codes have similarity between each other. In particular, the AMCD Multicultural Counseling Competencies and the IAMFC Ethical Codes have interactive issues when it comes to the preparation of culturally competent counselors and the intervention of a family counselor in a culturally competent manner.

We have seen this in the case of IAMFC Ethical Codes' challenge to members to "gain cultural competency, including awareness, knowledge, and skills to work with a diverse clientele." As mentioned earlier, this code is a direct call for members to engage in the process (awareness, knowledge, and skills) of becoming a multiculturally competent counselor. With IAMFC's code calling for the development of cultural competencies, we have an interactive interpretation.

Another way of looking at multiple counseling ethical codes is to use a *dimensional interpretation*. Dimensional structures have been suggested in the multicultural literature as being a contemporary and a more sophisticated way to look at the components of multicultural counseling (Wehrly, 1995). The stylistic model of transcultural counseling is an example of a dimensional interpretation. In this case, the model has separate constructs (dimensions) that interact with each other in a fashion that is best considered geometrical in nature. The interaction is made relational and visible by extending the constructs into the geometry. The geometry allows the reader to immediately see the interrelationship of the parts and to define the whole based on the relative positions of the parts. Wehrly (1995) suggested that dimensional structures can help counselors better understand complex multicultural systems. In this same way, complex interactions between ethical codes can be geometrically mapped. The geometry can provide the visual indicators of convergence or divergence in particular areas of content.

꙳ Multidimensional Interpretation ꙳

For the purpose of making sense out of the codes affecting culture, family, and career, a *multidimensional interpretation* is being used. A multidimensional interpretation uses the convergence of multiple geometrical shapes to best define the interrelationship of constructs, or in our case, ethical codes and competencies. One can look at a multidimensional interpretation and conceptualize the relationship as being interactive in some areas and restrictive in other areas. Multidimensional interpretation differs from linear interpretation in that the process in multidimensional interpretation extends itself to a fusion of all considered criteria, whereas the linear interpretation takes one criterion at a time. Built into the structure of a multidimensional interpretation can be linear interpretations, interactive interpretations, and dimensional interpretations. The smaller scale patterns have meaning within the larger context.

The easiest way to convey the dynamics of a dimensional interpretation is to present a model that fulfills the purpose of this chapter—to look at the integration of counseling ethical codes and competencies across the three disciplines of culture, family, and career. The only way to express the convergence of the three areas is to view it as a three-dimensional model. Figure 8.1 provides the reader with a dimensional interpretation that defines the convergence of culture, family, and career. Diagrammatically, this represents what is intended in this chapter to examine the relationship of these three counseling areas. The three counseling areas and their respective codes and competencies are represented diagrammatically as sectioned cylinders. The sections are superimposed on the cylinders to represent the three areas of cultural understanding, attitudes and beliefs, and knowledge and skills. Those three areas are defined by the AMCD competencies, but because they are present in the AMCD code we could expect to look for the same conceptual areas in the other codes, whether these constructs are a real parallel to or a reaction to the AMCD dimensions. The three codes are also spatially defined as cylinders to conceptualize a Venn diagram interaction between the three areas. Surrounding the three disciplines are umbrella codes that impact the provision of service to clients across the board.

From the multidimensional interpretation, certain relationships emerge and take on their own definitions on the basis of their relative relationship to other components. These relationships become entities of themselves, whether real components or conjectured components. Where all three codes coalesce in the center, the term adopted for this overlap of ethical codes is *convergent codes*. Convergent codes represent the clearest alignment of constructs among all areas considered. In a convergent situation, the same ethical construct would be represented in each of the ethical codes in the dimensional interpretation. *Complementary codes* are those codes that have two or more similarities among the disciplines but not all disciplines are included in this similarity. In Figure 8.1, complementary codes can be seen between AMCD

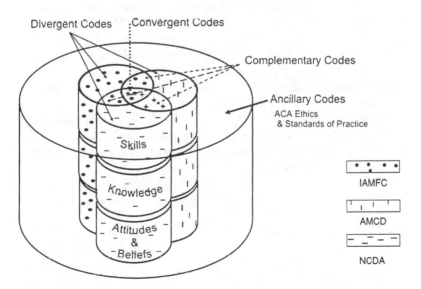

Figure 8.1. Three-dimensional interpretation of the convergence of the three counseling areas of culture, family, and career. IAMFC = International Association of Marriage and Family Counselors; AMCD = Association for Multicultural Counseling and Development; NCDA = National Career Development Association; ACA = American Counseling Association.

and IAMFC, AMCD and NCDA, and IAMFC and NCDA. *Divergent codes* represent those ethical codes and competencies that are unique to only one particular discipline. Divergent codes not only represent those content specific to a discipline but also potentially represent areas overlooked by other disciplines in the development of their codes and competencies. *Ancillary codes* are codes and competencies from external umbrella organizations that have an impact across the disciplines. In this case, ancillary codes are those from the *ACA Code of Ethics and Standards of Practice*. These codes coming from the larger association have quite a bit to contribute regarding client care, research, supervision, and the welfare of students. In addition, NCDA and IAMFC have based the structure of their codes to parallel ACA's code structure, so it is appropriate that they reside within a geometrical space surrounded by ACA.

The multidimensional structure is a dynamic process. As time changes and ethical codes are rewritten and competencies clarified, the structure of this diagram changes. It could be that a divergent code is picked up by another discipline and incorporated into their next revision of their ethical codes, in which case it would then be a complementary code with another discipline. Alternatively, each discipline might have something similar to say about the treatment of students that results in a convergent code among them. One would then foresee an eventual convergence of the three disciplines. Diagrammatically, it would appear as a single cylinder in which each discipline would have parallel inclusive codes. Besides being passively dynamic to the changes that occur in organizations, the multidimensional structure can be used as a planning tool for development of ethical codes or competencies in which there are areas lacking in one discipline. A discipline, NCDA for example, would do well to look at codes that are complementary between IAMFC and AMCD but may be a blind spot to NCDA. Responding to such gaps would provide members with a robust ethical code for their own discipline.

❧ Culture, Family, and Career Convergence ❦

When one looks specifically at the disciplines addressed in this book, the question becomes, "What codes are convergent among all three, complementary between two but not the third, and divergent that should be more convergent?" In general, there are few codes that are convergent between all three disciplines. Each discipline has included a statement or statements about sensitivity to diversity issues in their respective fields. Beyond this general statement about diversity, ethical codes addressing marriage and family work and career counseling do not extend themselves into the many contextual areas that these disciplines encroach. For example, in dealing with career issues, nothing is mentioned in the codes about blending of career and family. The NCDA Counseling Competencies do address the need for the counselor to be able to see the individual within the context of work–family balance. Similarly, in the IAMFC Ethical Codes, nothing is mentioned regarding work as it applies to family counseling issues despite career issues, and their impact on the family is often a symptom for seeking family counseling. In this way, career and family codes are divergent, and the IAMFC and NCDA may wish to look at how they could extend their codes to include more of these issues.

Conceptually, using Figure 8.1, associations need to develop more codes that are convergent in function. One could speculate that, given the scenario of associations scripting more convergent codes, the center convergent column would expand to extend itself filling into all three areas. As it expanded, there would be a decrease in divergent codes, by first becoming complementary codes and eventually convergent codes. The three distinct codes would begin to look more like each other, and the three columns in Figure 8.1 could coalesce into one large column containing the contents of all three codes. If associations further extended themselves into what we now see as ACA Ethics and Standards of Practice, the coalesced column would extend even further, encroaching on the whole cylinder.

ᔆ Training Standards ᔆ

The previous discussion assessed the ethical codes and competencies for the three areas of culture, family, and career. The ethical codes and competencies have developed in each of the associations over the years and are meant to act as guidelines for ethical and competent practice in a particular area of counseling. To ensure some basic consistency in the counselors' training for practice, the second focus of this chapter is on training standards for each of these fields.

The main provider of counseling training standards is CACREP, which accredits counseling programs at the master's and doctoral level. At the master's level, CACREP accredits programs in Community Counseling, School Counseling, College Counseling, Student Affairs Counseling, Career Counseling, Mental Health Counseling, Gerontological Counseling, and Marital, Couple, and Family Counseling (CACREP, 2000). At the doctoral level, CACREP accredits Counselor Education and Supervision doctoral programs. CACREP was incorporated in 1981 as the accrediting arm of the ACA. CACREP is viewed as an independent accrediting body from ACA, thereby allowing it to function autonomously and without fear of conflict of interest. CACREP is a partner in the accrediting community and maintains membership with the Association for Specialized and Professional

Accreditors, aligning itself with other accrediting agencies such as the Council on Rehabilitation Education, the American Psychological Association, and the National Counsel for Accreditation of Teacher Education.

A counselor education program would seek CACREP accreditation for its assurance of program quality. CACREP accreditation is both a process and a condition. The process of CACREP accreditation includes assessing the program's quality through compliance with specified educational standards. The condition of being accredited provides the public with assurance that the program is committed to particular standards established for quality control. CACREP provides organizational conditions (administration, class size, staffing patterns, and resource requirements) and curricular objectives that include eight core areas. In addition to organizational conditions and core curricular objectives, for those programs that wish to have a specialty area accreditation by CACREP, there are program area standards for each area. The adoption of program area standards gives the counselor education program the right to designate themselves as being CACREP accredited in that area.

Within the context areas of this book (culture, family, and career), CACREP has program objectives and curriculum for all programs in Social and Cultural Diversity and Career Development. CACREP has also identified program area standards for Career Counseling Programs and Marital, Couple, Family Counseling/Therapy Programs. Looking at the scope and magnitude as well as the convergence of standards will provide us with the extent that CACREP addresses training in these areas.

Table 8.1 provides an appended look at the CACREP program objectives and curriculum and program area standards of concern in this book. The left column contains program objectives and curriculum for Social and Cultural Diversity and Career Development. These objectives are part of what CACREP programs consider the core curriculum. Accredited programs must demonstrate that these content areas are covered through instruction or experience gained in the program. Each objective is often incorporated into a course curriculum objective of a specified course in the program of study. Generally, this emerges as a counselor education program having a course to cover each of the eight core curriculum.

With limited credit hours in a counselor education program and increasing demands for covering core curriculum areas, counselor education programs have developed some creative ways to manage the CACREP objectives. In some cases, two of the eight program objectives will be combined into one course when those program objectives dovetail. Another approach is an *integration model*, in which programs will take one curricular area and extend the objectives across multiple courses in the program. Because multiculturalism in counseling is historically the latest curricular development, many programs incorporate

Table 8.1

Abbreviated CACREP Program Objectives and Program Area Standards

PROGRAM OBJECTIVES AND CURRICULUM SOCIAL AND CULTURAL DIVERSITY	STANDARDS FOR MARITAL, COUPLE, AND FAMILY COUNSELING/ THERAPY PROGRAMS	STANDARDS FOR CAREER COUNSELING PROGRAMS
Studies that provide an understanding of the cultural context of relationships, issues, and trends in a multicultural and diverse society related to such factors as culture, ethnicity, nationality, age, gender, sexual orientation, mental and physical characteristics, education, family values, religious and spiritual values, socioeconomic status, and unique characteristics of individuals, couples, families, ethnic groups, and communities including all of the following:	A. FOUNDATIONS OF MARITAL, COUPLE, AND FAMILY COUNSELING/THERAPY 1. history/philosophy 2. structure and operations of professional organizations, preparation standards, and credentialing bodies 3. ethical and legal considerations 4. implications of professional issues unique to marital, couple, and family counseling/therapy including recognition, reimbursement, and right to practice 5. the role of marital, couple, and family counselors/therapists in a variety of practice settings and in relation to other helping professionals 6. the role of racial, ethnic, and cultural heritage, nationality, socioeconomic status, family structure, age, gender, sexual orientation, religious and spiritual beliefs,	A. FOUNDATIONS OF CAREER COUNSELING 1. history, philosophy, and trends in career counseling 2. settings for the practice of career counseling, including private and public sector agencies and institutions 3. roles, functions, and credentials 4. policies, laws, and regulations 5. professional organizations, competencies, and preparation standards 6. the role of racial, ethnic, and cultural heritage, nationality, socioeconomic status, family structure, age, gender, sexual orientation, religious and spiritual beliefs, occupation, and physical and mental status, and equity issues B. CONTEXTUAL DIMENSIONS OF CAREER COUNSELING Studies that provide an understanding of career counseling needs, the network of career services and resources available to individuals, and
a. multicultural and pluralistic trends, including characteristics and concerns between and within diverse groups nationally and internationally		
b. attitudes, beliefs, understandings, and acculturative experiences, including specific experiential learning activities		
c. individual, couple, family, group, and community strategies for working with diverse populations and ethnic groups		
d. counselors' roles in social justice, advocacy and conflict resolution, cultural self-		

(continued next page)

Table 8.1 (Continued)

Abbreviated CACREP Program Objectives and Program Area Standards

PROGRAM OBJECTIVES AND CURRICULUM SOCIAL AND CULTURAL DIVERSITY	STANDARDS FOR MARITAL, COUPLE, AND FAMILY COUNSELING/ THERAPY PROGRAMS	STANDARDS FOR CAREER COUNSELING PROGRAMS
awareness, the nature of biases, prejudices, processes of intentional and unintentional oppression and discrimination, and other culturally supported behaviors that are detrimental to the growth of the human spirit, mind, or body e. theories of multicultural counseling, theories of identity development, and multicultural competencies f. ethical and legal considerations Studies that provide an understanding of career development and related life factors, including all of the following: a. career development theories and decision-making models b. career; avocational, educational, occupational and labor market information resources, visual and print media, computer-based	occupation, physical and mental status, and equity issues **B. CONTEXTUAL DIMENSIONS OF MARITAL, COUPLE, AND FAMILY COUNSELING/THERAPY** 1. marital, couple, and family life-cycle dynamics, healthy family functioning, family structures, and development in a multicultural society, family of origin and intergenerational influences, cultural heritage, socioeconomic status, and belief systems 2. human sexuality issues and their impact on family and couple functioning, and strategies for their resolution 3. societal trends and treatment issues related to working with diverse family	the roles of career counselors as members of service provision teams, including all of the following: 1. knowledge of lifelong career needs of people throughout their education, employment, and retirement 2. knowledge of assessment and intervention strategies for career development and career counseling programs 3. knowledge of the continuum of formal and informal career counseling services and options 4. knowledge and skill in referring students and clients to appropriate mental health and career resources **C. KNOWLEDGE AND SKILL REQUIREMENTS FOR CAREER COUNSELOR** Career Development Theory, Individual and Group Counseling Skills, Individual and Group Assessment, Information Resources, Program Management and Implementation, Consultation,

career information systems, and other electronic career information systems

c. career development program planning, organization, implementation, administration, and evaluation

d. interrelationships among and between work, family, and other life roles and factors including the role of diversity and gender in career development

e. career and educational planning, placement, follow-up, and evaluation

f. assessment instruments and techniques that are relevant to career planning and decision making

g. technology-based career development applications and strategies, including computer-assisted career guidance and information systems and appropriate World Wide Web sites

h. career counseling processes, techniques, and resources, including those applicable to specific populations

i. ethical and legal considerations

systems (e.g., families in transition, dual-career couples, and blended families)

C. **KNOWLEDGE AND SKILL REQUIREMENTS FOR MARITAL, COUPLE, & FAMILY COUNSELOR/THERAPISTS**

1. family systems theories and other relevant theories and their application in working with couples and families, and other systems (e.g., legal legislative, school and community systems) and with individuals

2. interviewing, assessment, and case management skills for working with individuals, couples, families, and other systems; and implementing appropriate skill in systemic interventions

3. preventive approaches for working with individuals, couples, families, and other systems such as pre-marital counseling, parenting skills training, and relationship enhancement

4. specific problems that impede family functioning, including issues related to socioeconomic disadvantage, discrimination and bias, addictive behaviors, persona, and interventions for their resolution

5. research and technology applications in marital, couple, and family counseling/therapy

Specific Populations, Supervision, Ethical and Legal Issues, and Research and Evaluation are areas of knowledge and skill that have unique requirements for career counselors. These requirements are addressed in Section II, K.1-8 of the Core Curriculum, and Section III, Standards A through M, Clinical Instruction, of the CACREP Standards. However, Career Counselors require refined levels of knowledge and skill in all of these areas. Additionally, the following three (3) areas of career counseling knowledge and skill require the respective requirements noted here.

1. consultation
2. research and evaluation
3. ethical and legal issues

Note. Text portions with a single underline are complementary to Social and Cultural objectives; text portions with a double underline are complementary to Marital, Couple, and Family Counseling standards. CACREP = Council for Accreditation of Counseling and Related Educational Programs.

cultural issues throughout the other seven core areas. Those taking a full integration model of training on Social and Cultural Diversity do not have a separate course on cultural aspects of counseling. Faculty planning an integration model could argue that Social and Cultural Diversity best lends itself to the infusion throughout the curriculum and can be done so easier than integrating the other seven core areas. Students can then see the context of culture through various counseling subspecialties. Critics suggest that the integration model for this curriculum may not allow for adequate depth in training (Ridley, Mendoza, & Kanitz, 1994). Another faulty assumption is that all faculty are trained and prepared to include cultural issues into their content areas of teaching. With counselor educators in academia spanning the decades, many who are teaching may have never had a social and cultural diversity class as part of their own professional development. Using an integration model, the aforementioned faculty member would have to figure out how to incorporate diversity into his or her teaching without any academic training in multicultural counseling.

The most common program strategy for teaching multicultural counseling is to include it in the curriculum as a separate course. A separate course model allows for more time to be spent on the topic than the collective time found in the integration model but can result in a stigmatization of the content. Separate Social and Cultural Diversity courses could easily be viewed by students as distinct from the rest of the curriculum, as an added program requirement to satisfy professional social movement rather than a training experience with which they can develop a new set of counseling skills. Reynolds (1995) suggested that the best training experience uses a combination of a separate course and integration of cultural issues into the rest of the curriculum. In addition to having a separate course in multicultural counseling and infusing social and cultural diversity throughout the core, Reynolds suggested the inclusion of elective offerings on counseling special populations (e.g., Lesbian, Gay, and Bisexual Counseling; African American's in Counseling; and Counseling the Elderly).

Other core curriculum areas addressed by this book (career and family) are addressed in different ways by CACREP. CACREP recognizes Career Development as a core curriculum area. Career development as a field was one of the first clear counseling roles identified in personal guidance. Career development guidance has its roots back to the turn of the 20th century with Frank Parsons establishing a career guidance process for counselors. Career development counseling maintains its discipline in counseling and is still considered a core curricular area despite recent evidence indicating counselors from CACREP-accredited programs perceive career counseling as the least valuable aspect of their graduate training to their professional practice (McGlothlin, 2001).

Counseling issues specific to families and couples are not considered part of the core curriculum established by CACREP. Counseling as a profession emerged from a personal guidance and individual focus and only recently has recognized the impact of family systems from a curricular area. The decision to include family systems in the general core curriculum of a counselor education program is not one that is driven by CACREP requirements. CACREP programs that include family counseling courses often include them as an elective for students, rarely as part of the requirements for graduation and in some cases not even as an available elective. In this case, there is a great disparity between what the counseling curriculum prepares a student for and what the student faces in most clinical settings. Counseling graduates have to work with families more now than in the past, and without family counseling theory as part of their core, they would graduate inadequately prepared for practice. Similar arguments for including substance abuse counseling as the core curriculum for counseling programs could be made based on the prevalence of addiction issues clients typically bring to a counselor (Fisher & Harrison, 2000).

Table 8.1 also includes the program area standards for programs that CACREP gives accreditation in and programs that are reflective of the areas defined by this book. The two CACREP program areas covered in this book are Marital, Couple, and Family Counseling/Therapy and Career Counseling. Table 8.1 includes annotated descriptions of the standards for these areas broken down into (A) Foundations, (B) Contextual Dimensions, and (C) Knowledge and Skill Requirements. A fourth component (D) is the Clinical Instruction required for each program area standard. From Table 8.1, under the Foundations component, one can see the similar foundational constructs that exist between the Career Counseling and Marital, Couple, and Family Counseling/Therapy (arrows signifying similar constructs). The Foundations component appears to include similar constructs of history, philosophy, professional organizations and credentialing, practice settings, ethics, and the role diversity plays in practice. The second component, Contextual Dimensions, include standards that are context specific to the specialization area and, for that reason, one does not find a great deal of convergence between the two program areas. For Marital, Couple, and Family Counseling, the contextual elements are related to family structures, human sexuality issues, and societal trends in treatment (including diverse family systems). For Career Counseling, those contextual elements include a network of career services, life-span career needs, assessment and intervention strategies, formal and informal career counseling, and referral skills. The third component involves looking at the Knowledge and Skill Requirements of these two specialty areas. Once again the elements have little convergence in that they represent specific knowledge and skills necessary for competency in this specialty area. Included in the Marital, Couple, and Family Counseling standards are knowledge and skill elements regarding application of theory to working with clients; interviewing, assessment, and case management; preventative approaches for working with clients; specific family problem areas; and research and technology applications in family counseling. Knowledge and skill elements required for Career Counseling include refined levels of knowledge of career development theory; counseling skills as they relate to career; assessment; program management and resources; specific populations; and supervision. In addition, the standards call for career counselors to have knowledge and skill in consultation, research and evaluation, and ethical and legal issues.

The CACREP program areas of Marital, Couple, and Family Counseling and Career Counseling have clinical instruction standards. In both cases, the clinical instruction consists of a 600-clock hour internship occurring in a setting that can provide the student with client contact specific to their specialization. This requirement includes a minimum of 240 direct service clock hours. The internship occurs under the supervision of a clinical supervisor as defined by the CACREP standards (minimum of a master's degree and appropriate license in the field and 2 years professional experience in the program area with which the student is completing their clinical instruction).

෨ Convergence of Training Standards ෪

One would not expect to see much convergence between training standards for such diverse areas as culture, family, and career. Table 8.1 has underlined portions of the program objectives and program standards in these three areas that converge. Because there is no program area designated for Multicultural Counseling, we cannot readily identify convergence with the other two areas. As mentioned, there appears to be a complementary relationship between the foundations' components of Career Counseling and Marital, Couple, and Family Counseling. Other areas of complementarity can be seen throughout Table 8.1 by identifying those portions of standards and program objectives that are underlined. Text portions underlined with a single underline are complementary to Social and Cultural Diversity objectives. Those text portions underlined with a double underline are complementary to Marital, Couple, and Family Counseling standards. There were no apparent standards or objectives that were complementary to Career Counseling found within the context of the other program areas.

One could argue for greater convergence of training standards similar to the convergence found in ethical standards, but the intent of training standards are different. Training standards are created to establish discrete portions of knowledge and skills that a student is to master for a given specialty. Because training standards are so closely linked to competencies, and competencies in counseling subspecialties are defining characteristics of the subspecialty, one might expect them to be less convergent across subspecialties. The CACREP program objectives are just the baseline for what kinds of training experiences counseling students need to gain. The AMCD with the publication of the MCC has raised the level of expectation within this concentration area. CACREP and ACA would do well to endorse programs that can establish training based on the MCC and to encourage other professionals to establish comprehensive competencies for their specialty area.

The future of training standards will likely be in the direction of establishing "best practices" for the subspecialties. As an example, the Association for Specialists in Group Work (1998) has established a set of best practices for those members who are doing group work. Once the *practice* of the specialty has been defined, then the establishment of best practice *training* methods would follow. Best practices and best training methods should be established based on research support. The Association for Counselor Education and Supervision Multicultural Counseling Interest Network (2001) recently included on their agenda the development of best training practices for multicultural education. It will be interesting to see how these best training practices become actualized and whether they are established by supported research outcomes versus personal preference in training.

❧ Improving Training and Practice ❧

As counselors, we strive to become better at what we do in the desire to be more effective with our clients. Counselor educators look for ways to improve the training of counselors and establish an effective pedagogy in the counselor education field. Where does one get new ideas for practice and training? Listed below are just a few suggestions where one can obtain new ideas for improving their training and practice.

1. Literature
   Counselors and counselor educators need to watch the current literature for new ideas on practice and training methods. Sometimes I find it useful to browse through old journals to refresh ideas regarding training and practice. This quick retrospective often sparks ideas that did not occur the first time I read the journal.
2. Conferences
   A second source for good ideas on practice and training methods is to attend professional conferences. A review of the presentations at a conference will often find titles related to "best practices" or

opportunities for counselors and counselor educators to "resource share" ideas about teaching and practice.

3. Listservs

There are electronic mailing lists, or listservs, which are resource-sharing vehicles for counselors looking to improve their practice and counselor educators looking to improve counseling training methods. The Counselor Education and Supervision NETwork Listserv, or CESNET-L, which I developed, has grown to become an online resource for sharing training ideas. CESNET-L is available at http://listserv.kent.edu/archives/cesnet-l.html

4. Internet

A search of the Internet using Web-browser search engines yields a great deal of information about counseling practices and teaching strategies. Many counselor education programs have their program information and syllabi on the Web, yielding a wealth of information and ideas for counselors and counselor educators.

5. Collaboration

Given the complex combination of counseling specialty areas covered in this book (culture, family, and career), it is unlikely that one person would hold the knowledge for three specialty areas. This is where selective collaboration can come to your assistance. Encouraged is collaboration with other experts outside of your content specialty to develop new and innovative ways of converging specialty areas. The three editors involved in this book exemplify the collaboration from three distinct content specialties of culture, family, and career.

6. Consultants

Many counselor education programs, especially prior to an accreditation visit, will bring in outside program consultants to survey the program for weaknesses and suggest means to rectify the weakness. Do not underestimate the value that having an outside eye on the counselor training program of clinical practice can have on correcting holes in training or flaws in service delivery.

7. Program Evaluation

All program evaluation does not have to be done by hired consultants. Some of the most valuable information can be gathered along the way from students in training programs or clients in counseling settings. Establishing methods for client and student feedback and ways in which the information will be used is often a standard part of clinical practice and teaching environments. Because many counseling work environments require obtaining this kind of information for program evaluation, it is senseless not to have a means to consider and implement those ideas gathered from the feedback.

👒 Summary 👒

Culture, family, and career (who we are, where we came from, and what we do) seem so closely intertwined in the person as a whole it is hard to imagine trying to understand a client's context without trying to understand each one of these components. Although we as counselors intuitively know that these contextual components uniquely interact in the person, from an ethical code and training standards point of view, we largely see these as separate entities instead of interactive components. To understand these as active, dynamic components that influence each other, we will have to think of ethical codes and training standards as being multidimensional and fluid. As we begin to revise these standards, we support a better representation of the interaction of these components.

👒 References 👒

Arredondo, P., & Glauner, T. (1992). *Personal dimensions of identity model*. Boston: Empowerment Workshops.

Arredondo, P., Toporek, R., Brown, S. P., Jones, J., Locke, D. C., Sanchez, J., & Stadler, H. (1996a). Operationalization of the multicultural counseling competencies. *Journal of Multicultural Counseling and Development, 24,* 42-78.

Arredondo, P., Toporek, R., Brown, S. P., Jones, J., Locke, D. C., Sanchez, J., & Stadler, H. (1996b). *Operationalization of the multicultural counseling competencies*. Alexandria, VA: Association for Multicultural Counseling and Development.

Association for Counselor Education and Supervision Multicultural Counseling Interest Network. (2001, March). Minutes of the meeting held at the American Counseling Association World Conference, San Antonio, TX.

Association for Specialist in Group Work. (1998). *Principles for diversity-competent group workers*. Retrieved from http://asgw.educ.kent.edu/diversity.htm

Brown, M. T., & Landrum-Brown, J. (1995). Counselor supervision: Cross-cultural perspectives. In J. Ponterotto, J. Casas, L. Suzuki, & C. Alexander (Eds.), *Handbook of multicultural counseling* (pp. 263-286). Thousand Oaks, CA: Sage.

Carter, R. T., & Swanson, J. L. (1990). The validity of the Strong Interest Inventory with Black Americans: A review of the literature. *Journal of Vocational Behavior, 36,* 195-209.

Council for Accreditation of Counseling and Related Educational Programs. (2000). *CACREP accreditation manual of the Council for Accreditation of Counseling and Related Educational Programs* (1st ed.). Alexandria, VA: Author.

Fisher, G. L., & Harrison, T. C. (2000). *Substance abuse: Information for school counselors, social workers, therapists, and counselors*. Boston: Allyn & Bacon.

International Association of Marriage and Family Counselors. (2001). *IAMFC ethical codes* [Draft]. Retrieved from http://www.iamfc.org/ethicalcodes.htm

McFadden, J. (1999). *Transcultural counseling* (2nd ed.). Alexandria, VA: American Counseling Association.

McGlothlin, J. M. (2001). *CACREP: An evaluation of the perceived benefit of core curriculum standards to professional practice.* Unpublished doctoral dissertation, Ohio University.

National Career Development Association. (2000a). *Career counseling competencies* (Revised 1997 ed.). Retrieved from http://www.ncda.org/about/polccc.html

National Career Development Association. (2000b). *National Career Development Association ethical standards* (Revised 1991 ed.). Retrieved from http://www.ncda.org/about/poles.html

Reynolds, A. L. (1995). Challenges and strategies for teaching multicultural counseling courses. In J. G. Ponterotto, J. M. Casas, L. A. Suzuki, & C. M. Alexander (Eds.), *Handbook of multicultural counseling* (pp. 312–330). Thousand Oaks, CA: Sage.

Ridley, C. R., Mendoza, D. W., & Kanitz, B. E. (1994). Multicultural training: Reexamination, operationalization, and integration. *Counseling Psychologist, 22,* 227–289.

Sue, D., Arredondo, P., & McDavis, R. (1992). Multicultural counseling competencies and standards: A call to the profession. *Journal of Multicultural Counseling and Development, 20,* 64–88.

Wehrly, B. (1995). *Pathways to multicultural counseling competence: A developmental journey.* Pacific Grove, CA: Brooks/Cole.

❧ Index ❧

ethical codes, 140–46
improving training and practice, 159–60
interpreting multiple codes in a
single context, 146–48
multidimensional interpretation, 148–50
training standards, 151–58
Counselor Education and
Supervision NETwork
Listserv (CESNET-L), 160
Cox, R. D., 80
CPSS (Context, Phase, Stage, and
Style) model, 98
Cramer, S. H., 6, 7
Crane, D. R., 50
cultural sensitivity, in multicultural
family counseling, 5
culture and career issues, 126–29
culture-conflict family, 82

Dawis, R. V., 36, 37, 45–46, 47
Day, S. X., 42
deShazer, Steve, 52
dimensional interpretation of ethical codes, 147–48
discrimination, influences in
career development, 8
racism and exclusion in the
workplace, 105
divergent ethical codes, 150
dual-career/dual-earner families, 5,
10–11
dual-career marriages, 80
dual-career women, reentry, 104
Dunkle, J. H., 128

Education of All Handicapped
Children Act of 1975, 49
enmeshment, 51
Enright, M. S., 130
epistemology, 20–21

Epp, L. R., 12
Erickson, Milton, 51, 52
ethical codes, 140–46
ethnic populations in the U.S.,
definition of family structure
in, 4, 5
Ethnicity and Family
(McGoldrick, Giordano, and
Pearce), 12
European American counselors,
107–8
constructive developmental
stage of, 110
gender roles of, 109
intersections between client's
and counselor's contexts, 112
middle class backgrounds of,
109–10
"normal" family life, 108–9
traditional counseling
approaches of, 110–12
European American families,
issues for, 8–10
Evans, K. M., 124
extended families, 5, 100

family, redefined, 4–5
family career counseling
career counseling and families,
10–12
multicultural competencies in,
5–6
Family Educational Rights and
Privacy Act of 1974, 49
family issues
and Holland's theory, 42
and Krumboltz's theory, 44–45
and Super's theory, 39
and TWA, 47
family life and career counseling,
125–26
family life cycle, changes in, 5
family life stories, 26–29